Georgia
Ghosts

Georgia Ghosts

ISBN: 1-58173-508-1

Book design by Pat Covert

Printed in the United States of America

Georgia Ghosts

they are among us

Ian Alan

SWEET
WATER
PRESS

Table of Contents

They Are Among Us

They Are Among Us

My name is Ian Alan. Among other things, I collect ghosts. My fascination with ghosts, phantoms, and other unbidden guests began as a small child in Louisiana. This is a place known for strange and mysterious happenings. Nearly everyone had a family story that revolved around the supernatural.

Our household was no different, for we had two ghosts who subtly affected our lives. One was an elderly woman who had died in the house long before we moved in. We regarded her with great respect. She often warned us of small calamities and childhood dangers that were about to happen. Occasionally, in more mischievous moments, she would rearrange the canned goods and pots in my mother's kitchen. As annoying as that could be, everyone in our family regarded her as a protective and benevolent spirit. Our other guest was quite the opposite.

I was the only member of my family who could see the man clad in dark clothes that hung on him like a heavy winter coat. Still, we could sense his presence, and it made us all uncomfortable. It became clear very early on that the old woman was there to protect us from the dark man as they battled in the shadows for stewardship over the family. It was in this environment that I learned to see, speak to, and interact with ghosts.

In ensuing years I traveled all over the globe tracking and "catching" phantoms employing techniques that could isolate, make visible, and even banish malevolent spirits. More often, I was merely a witness to the spirits and their timeless activities. The spirit world is a viable dimension that intersects with our own. The activity of ghosts can tell us just as much about ourselves as living beings as it can about what occurs after we are no longer living.

No place on earth is this more true than in the southern United States. Spectral tales dramatically underscore every facet of life in the American South. From the founding through the Civil War to modern times, ghosts and spirits have been a vital part of our Southern culture. For more than 200 years, they have shaped and influenced us, and I have often wondered if we would be truly comfortable knowing the extent of their influence. Surely that is a question that each of us must answer on our own.

As you read the stories and true accounts that follow, ask yourself if there have been moments in your life when something other than your Savior has guided or moved you this way or that. Moments of intuition, feelings of dread, warnings that appeared out of nowhere, and more palpable events have traditionally been the language that ghosts employ to communicate with the living. Occasionally, they resort to visitation as a way to get our attention.

Have you seen someone who is out of place or recollected a conversation that you can't remember having with anyone living? Well, many people have experienced these things, and much, much more. Read on and ask yourself, "Could this ever happen to me?" I can tell you from experience that if you live or travel in the South, sooner or later, you will meet at least one of our ghosts. Sometimes it will be a kind spirit while other times well ... not so kind. What will you take away from the experience—that is, if you are allowed to leave?

Ian Alan

The Ghosts
of Andersonville

The Ghosts of Andersonville

Charlie Martin was still a young man and the pride and joy of his Atlanta diocese. He had become a priest partly to rebel against his atheistic and overly educated parents. They were both college professors and dedicated to the rational mind. The last thing they wanted was a son who was a clergyman.

But now as he drove down Highway 49 in southern Georgia, Charlie angrily wondered if he ought to change careers, not a small feat for a Catholic priest. There was no question that he was called to the religious life, but even after he had been ordained, he still couldn't handle the politics and wrangling of the church.

The bishop who oversaw Charlie's parish was as overbearing and smothering as his parents. Only two days ago during Charlie's yearly review, the bishop had criticized Charlie's work. It was the kind of polite and brutal dressing down that his parents specialized in—full of smiles and condescension. Just thinking about it made his blood boil.

"Father Martin, you simply have to wise up," the bishop proclaimed, "and expand your mental wings. Your spiritual framework is much too narrow my boy. Go beyond it. Walk away from your ivory tower and experience what happens to real people." There was just enough truth in the old bishop's words to make them hurt. Maybe he was a failure as a priest. As he pulled off the highway to take a break from the driving, Charlie couldn't get over the feeling that he was holding onto something that had wilted.

For some reason Charlie couldn't explain, he had followed a line of cars off the exit ramp and into a parking lot. He desperately needed some rest, and this tourist trap was as good a spot as any. Only after he was out of the car and stretching his legs did he realize that he was at Andersonville.

Most southerners learned about Andersonville prison when they were in junior high or high school. To Father Charlie, though, the story of this notorious military stockade was something that he would have preferred not to know about.

During the Civil War, the Confederate army used this site to confine captured Union army troops. Between February 1864 and April 1865, almost 50,000 prisoners were detained there, but the prison had only been built to hold a fraction of that number. Charlie reflected on the horror and despair of the prisoners who slept on the ground covered in maggots, filth, and vermin.

Inadequate food and dirty water led to epidemics

within the camp. Almost 14,000 died of diseases like scurvy and dysentery. Charlie couldn't decide if it was the heat of the sun, the events of the week, fatigue, or the tragic memories trapped all around that made him feel uncomfortable. All he really knew was that he felt sick.

Charlie had been too preoccupied with his stomach to notice the tall lanky priest approaching him. Before he knew it, the older cleric had popped open a large umbrella and used it to shade them both. The sudden movement and the closeness of the tall priest startled him briefly, but he was grateful for the kind gesture and coolness of the shade.

"You looked like you needed a little protection from the sun, young man," he said. Charlie couldn't get over how foggy and unsteady he felt. He knew that he needed to clear his head, especially now with the old priest pressing him for conversation.

"You best loosen that collar, son. There's nothing worse than a black shirt and cleric collar on a hot day like today," said the priest.

"Thanks," replied Charlie. Smiling in agreement, he began loosening his collar. "My name is Charlie Martin. Thanks for the shade."

"My pleasure, Charlie. Old priests have to stick together." He punctuated his remark with a sly wink and knobby elbow jabbed lightly into Charlie's ribs.

"Slow down, Father," Charlie said, "I'm not that old. Not yet, anyway."

"You are older than you think, Charlie," said the old man. "If you've come to this place, then you're an old soul, that's for certain. I've spent most of my life in these parts. I come here most every week since they made it a national historic site in 1970. Every time I'm here, I see at least one or two old souls, sometimes more."

The "old soul" talk was a little odd for a Catholic priest, but Charlie didn't care. He was beginning to feel better than he had for days. Despite his odd demeanor and out-dated black suit, shoes, and umbrella, the old priest was confident and peaceful. Just standing next to him was like sitting on the bank of a calm lake. For the first time since he parked the car, Charlie noticed how very blue the sky was. It seemed funny that he hadn't noticed before.

They both stood silent for a moment before the old priest spoke again. "You've got to trust in the future, my boy. Brighter days are ahead. No matter what you've been going through, it'll work out."

Charlie was a little shocked and amazed by the old man's perception. Still, it was obvious that they had a connection. It was that sense of connection that encouraged him to start talking about his troubles.

Charlie talked about the bishop and his parents. He talked about feeling trapped as a priest in a big city parish and his desire to help people. At first his words were heartfelt and authentic, but then he began to complain. Complaining soon turned to selfishness and indulgence. The old man turned confessor listened intently at first, that is, until Charlie began to gush emotionally in forced concern for his fellow man.

Charlie felt an odd tingling in his scalp that distracted him. It was then that he noticed anger in the old priest's eyes. All of a sudden, the sky wasn't quite as blue as it had been.

"How dare you come to this place and talk about feeling trapped! Real men were trapped here. This is a real prison, not one created in your mind! I'll tell you the truth," he said as he looked over the cemetery, "if you don't give wings to your soul, you will lose it in this place."

Charlie felt his knees wobble, and he began to be aware of people milling around the park. He was about to look around, but his eyes remained fixed on the tall man with the umbrella.

"How many confessions can you bear to hear?" the dark man said. "How many times a day can you give a dying and broken soldier the Last Rites? There are just too many of them. Can you see them, Charlie? They're all here."

Charlie looked around but couldn't see anything. In fact, there wasn't a tourist or visitor in sight.

"Look, Charlie. Do you see them? This is my parish. Nope, there wasn't a chaplain at this place before my bishop sent me here. June 16. That was my first day. A glorious day!"

It was then that Charlie noticed a horrible odor, a stench that seemed to rise all at once from the ground itself. The stench made his knees wobble even more. His head began to spin. The only thing he could see clearly was the old priest gesturing with a bony finger and speaking with a booming voice. "The dead house is over there with men stacked like firewood. There are so many waiting their turn. Can you help these souls, Charlie?"

The old priest leaned in closely as Charlie looked up. The old man pressed his long finger into Charlie's forehead and, for Father Charlie Martin at least, everything changed.

Everything was different, and perhaps for the first time in his life, Charlie's eyes were opened, and he began to see things as they really were. The clean and organized reverence of a national historic site dropped away to reveal the chaos of decay and the irreverence of a war that threw brother against brother. The dead and the dying were everywhere he looked. Modern colors were replaced by the monotone of a long forgotten place and time. The only thing that he could smell was death.

"My bishop sent me here," said the dark man, "because I'd been a prisoner for a time up north. At first, I was angered and desolated by this place, but then I realized that we are all prisoners. This is where I belong, Charlie. From that first day in June, it has been my home, and these souls have been my flock."

Charlie frantically rubbed his eyes. He couldn't believe what he was seeing. There were hundreds of things that had once been men slowly walking toward him. Remnants of flesh and torn clothing hung from exposed bone. The old priest pressed him to his knees with one hand while the other still held the black umbrella upward blocking the sun.

"So many souls to tend to, Father Martin. All of them trapped men, all of them in prison, all of us in prison." The specter looked at Charlie with black eyes and said, "Do you feel trapped enough to join us, Father Martin?"

Charlie was stunned and couldn't do anything but stare at the wraith.

"Father Charlie Martin," he demanded, "could Andersonville be your next parish?"

The dead prisoners were close enough to touch Charlie. He fell backward on the ground as they reached for him, and then, as he never had before, Charlie screamed for his life.

"Whoa there, Father!" a frightened voice said. "Take

it easy." Charlie found himself sitting on a bench with a groundskeeper standing over him. The dead house was gone. The ghosts that were upon him had also vanished, as did the old priest that had held him to his knees. The sun was shining, and the foul stench that had invaded his nose was fading.

"Are you okay, Father?" the man said. "You looked like you were having a bad time of it."

Charlie took a deep breath and rubbed his face to prove to himself that he really was awake, and it had all been a bad dream. He nervously told the groundskeeper about his nightmare in great detail. It had all seemed so real.

It was then that the groundskeeper smiled and said, "Son, you've just met Father Whelan. He came to the stockade in 1864, and some say that he never left. Those of us who work around here catch a glimpse of him from time to time with his big umbrella and dark suit. But he only gets close to other priests. Everyone else thinks he's more comfortable with other men of the cloth. But me, I think he goes wherever he's needed."

Charlie got into his car, left the Andersonville Historic Site, and headed north. As he drove back to Atlanta, he pondered the notion that we are all in a prison of one sort or another. Days earlier, he would've told you that he himself was trapped. Today, however, he felt freer than he ever had in his life.

19

Lost Gold of the Confederacy

Lost Gold of the Confederacy

In his younger days, Gordy Franks had been a bit of a rogue. He had frequented loud parties and would go anywhere a crowd of people gathered to kill a few brain cells with excess smoke and drink. Now, well into his sixties, Gordy was a loner. Loud gatherings and crowds of people no longer attracted him.

These days Gordy described himself as a treasure hunter, but most of the folks in Wilkes County knew him as a wandering junk collector. This characterization was just fine with Gordy because he knew that one man's junk was another man's "find of the century." Besides, no one bothered him, and he got to be alone in the great outdoors.

He had learned to create art from other people's cast-offs and sold them at small county fairs and flea markets throughout Georgia. It had grown into quite a business over the last few years. In fact, it was getting harder and harder to find good junk to keep the business going. This didn't bother Gordy one bit because, the truth be known, he enjoyed the challenge and solitude of the hunt more than anything else. People, by and large, left him alone when he was in the woods, back alleys, and

22

junkyards looking for stuff. Some said he had sold his pride for peace and quiet. He sometimes wondered if they might be right. But then, the notion that he might discover something really special in his wanderings pushed the idea from his mind. On one occasion, though, he found more than he bargained for.

Gordy had listened to stories about the lost Confederate gold all of his life. Every old timer that recounted the tale had his own way of telling it. Legend has it that during the dark end days of the Civil War, when things were going from bad to worse for the South, the gold reserves of the Confederacy were secreted away in Washington, Georgia. The Union army was able to locate some of it hidden in a local bank, but the bulk of it was buried somewhere in the county. Unwilling to let the gold fall into Union hands, the Confederate soldiers who buried it took great pains to hide its location. They also took the secret to their graves.

Several attempts to find the gold were mounted but to no avail. Rumor had it that the young southern captain whose mission it was to hide the gold left ingenious clues to the site's location. But if he had, those too were hidden.

By now, tales of the lost Confederate treasure were permanently interwoven into local legend. Occasionally, someone would talk of seeing ghostly riders searching the woods. Sometimes they were Yankees and at other times Rebels, but always the storyteller emphasized that the gold was never found and that the specters are still searching to this day. Gordy didn't much care for the tales. With all the time he spent out of doors, if he hadn't seen the ghost riders, then as far as he was concerned, they didn't exist.

One night, after hours at a county fair, Gordy and a group of traveling artists and vendors watched an old Choctaw Indian do a dance supposedly designed to summon the spirits of the dead Rebels. The Indian was a good Christian, as the old-timers say, and preceded his dance with a church hymn and a prayer delivered in his native Choctaw language. The dance itself consisted largely of his walking in circles around the campfire that inevitably gets built at small county fairs.

More hymns, prayers, and circles later, no ghosts had appeared, so everyone finished their beers and went to bed. Gordy clapped the Choctaw on his back. "Better luck next time, Chief," he said. The Indian shrugged and replied, "Sometimes the magic works, and sometimes it doesn't." They both laughed and went off to their campsites.

Gordy needed his sleep. The fairgoers would begin showing up early the next morning. For some reason, he couldn't drift off to sleep. Maybe he was getting too old to sleep on the ground anymore. He asked himself if it might not be time to trade in his sleeping bag for a camper or pop-up like the other traveling artists had done. Gordy thought better of it; a camper would be one more thing that he'd have to drag around. He rolled over and let his mind ramble on to other things.

Gordy was just about to drift off to sleep when everything in the campground suddenly went silent. There were no sounds at all. He could hear no frogs, no crickets, or katydids, just silence. From his reclined position, he caught sight of what appeared to be smoke or fog entering the campground moving from east to west. This seemed strange because the night breeze was blowing west to east. Gordy was unable to fully appreciate the mystery of a fog that moves against the wind because he had noticed something even stranger—the fog glowed!

The swirling mist didn't blanket the campground like an earthly fog would do. Rather, it cut a meandering path in and around the individual campsites like some sort of trail. Part of that trail came within inches of Gordy's face.

Gordy tried to move but couldn't. In his younger days, he hadn't been afraid of anything, but now he was practically quaking in fear. What he witnessed next froze him motionless to the ground. A lone horseman appeared at the foggy trailhead slowly entering the campground. His horse had probably been a flashy mover once, but now its hooves fell deliberately with an unadorned "thud."

The rider sat tall and surveyed the sleeping campers. He was dressed in the uniform of an officer in the Confederate army, in fact, a captain. A broken saber hung from his hand as he moved with the fog weaving in and out of the sites. Periodically, the rider would stop and extend his sword toward the ground. He moved its broken tip slowly left and right. Gordy thought the rider looked like a dowser searching for water, but he knew that it was really a ghost looking for his gold.

Gordy closed his eyes tightly, hoping that the apparition would go away. He lay still for several minutes before he had enough courage to see if the rider had gone. When he opened his eyes, he discovered that the dead Rebel captain had dismounted and was standing right next to him.

With ancient boots only inches from his face, Gordy tried to look upward, but his neck muscles simply wouldn't work. It was then that the soldier leaned forward toward the ground in front of Gordy and began poking and probing the earth with the broken end of his saber. After six or seven thrusts, he stopped and straightened up. Gordy's eyes caught a glint of polished

26

metal flashing from the disturbed earth. Then he saw it; a roughly minted gold coin slowly floated upward from the soil and through the glowing fog. Gordy watched the coin as it rose. The sight of it transfixed him.

As the horse soldier reached out and grabbed the coin, Gordy noticed, for the first time, that the captain was a skeleton. No flesh could be seen, at all. Only bone polished by the elements remained in the gray uniform. The wraith held the coin closely to his face. Gordy imagined that he saw pain in the skull's permanent death grin. Then in a rasping voice that seemed to come from the fog, Gordy heard the rider say, "It's pure. I'm almost home." Gordy simply couldn't take any more of the fright. He closed his eyes tightly and began humming the Choctaw's church hymn he had heard earlier. He was shaking uncontrollably, and though he'd always enjoyed good health, he wondered if he might be having a heart attack.

The next morning, Gordy awoke to normal sights and sounds. The sun was up, and people busied themselves making breakfast and preparing for the last day of the fair. The aroma of bacon and coffee filled the air, and someone was playing a guitar. He wasn't sure what had happened the previous night. Did he really see a ghost? Was it possible that he had bunked near a clue to the hidden Confederate gold? No tracks remained from either the horse or pale rider, yet the ground where Gordy had been sleeping was disturbed as if someone were digging about for something. Could it have been the ghost of the Rebel captain? Gordy decided to stop thinking about it and quietly chalked up the whole event as a bad dream.

Later that day, people filed past his booth admiring his junk creations. But Gordy was too distracted to pay them much attention. He just couldn't get the images of the fog and horse soldier out of his mind. Then there was the wild thought that the hidden gold really did exist and was waiting to be found by some determined treasure hunter.

A few moments later, Gordy saw the Choctaw Indian amongst the fairgoers walking in his direction. He called the man aside and quietly started to tell him what he had experienced. But before he completely jumped into the story, Gordy abruptly stopped talking. Perhaps it would be better to keep the whole event a secret.

After all, there was gold buried somewhere out among the woods and old plantations of Washington, Georgia. It was just the kind of treasure that Gordy Franks waited his whole life to find, and he didn't need anybody's help searching for it. After all, truth be told, he liked the challenge of the hunt and the solitude more than anything else.

The College Séance

The College Séance

Very few of the students who attend Augusta College know of its unique and colorful history. Several of the buildings that now make up the college were part of a federal arsenal before the Civil War. At the outbreak of the War Between the States, it was seized by the Confederacy and soon became a center of Confederate military activity in that part of the South.

Fighting Joe Wheeler of the Confederate army clashed with General Sherman on these college campus grounds, and the Augusta Arsenal Cemetery is filled with both northern and southern soldiers who fought each other, died together, and are buried together at the cemetery.

Tom Scott, an English major at Augusta College, didn't know anything about this history, like most of the students at the college, and frankly, he didn't care. Tom was a partier by today's standards. He reveled in life— mostly the social life of college. Everyone looking at him would say he was emotionally very secure, but that just masked a much deeper insecurity. He was a smart boy. He knew how to enjoy the moment and how to have a good time. But deep inside, he was restless, and it was this unconscious restlessness that drove him from one activity to another.

Tom Scott was the kind of guy who would hang out with his friends as long as they were laughing and joking and having a good time. He was in there with them. But as soon as a deep conversation came up about school, politics, or any subject that wasn't superficial, he would zone out. He'd pick up a rubber band or a drinking straw or a pen and amuse himself until the heavy conversation had passed, and he could get on to some serious fun and some serious partying.

Fundamentally, Tom was a very strong individual, and he had amazing resources that most people couldn't see. He was intelligent. He could read something once and grasp whatever he was reading very, very quickly. But mostly he was inspired by his unconscious mind. He would often leap to brave actions or sometimes foolhardy actions because he trusted his intuition. He had a simple phrase he lived by: Every morning when he woke up, he would say, "Today, I trust myself."

Unfortunately, most of it was a sham. From the outside, everyone saw him as a very self-assured and a very calm person. But inside, Tom thought himself a coward, and he forced himself into emotional isolation. His peaceful demeanor was really a sham. It didn't matter where Tom was, what college, what job, or what relationship he was in, he always felt stuck. He could keep things calm and on an even keel because of his gregarious nature, but he knew that deep down inside keeping things calm didn't mean that he was at peace.

Everything was going along just fine for Tom at college. He had majored in English because everyone in the fine arts department seemed cool to him, and frankly, he didn't know what else to major in. Truth be known, he would probably change majors five or six times before he actually graduated from college, that is, if he ever graduated at all.

The day was a typical day for Tom. He was relaxing and enjoying himself, drawing on his ability to have a good time no matter where he was, when he met Barbara. To the other students at Augusta College, Barbara was known as "The Empress."

She was called that because, well, among other things, she had what the old-timers would call "The Shining," or "A Key." The Shining meant she had a special ability that allowed her to shine light on the dark or hidden side of existence. To call her a Key meant that she could unlock the doors to the other worlds, to the spirit worlds and the afterlife. She'd been like this since she was very young.

Barbara possessed an insight into the eternal cycle of life and growth and death. She could take a look at somebody and, in an instant, size him or her up. Did they need to be reborn? Could the spirit world help them? Did they just need to be renewed? Or do they need to be put on a different path of growth and development?

Barbara had the ability to tell all of this at an instant, and the first time she saw Tom Scott, she smiled. She knew this was somebody who could really use her help. The very first time they struck up a conversation, Barbara said to him, "Tom, you look like a boy who's in desperate need of a séance."

Tom Scott was intrigued and just a little bit frightened as well.

Now, every native southerner knows exactly what you need for a good séance. But Tom was from up north, Ohio to be precise, and the folks in Akron didn't have any idea what it took to conduct a good séance. But Barbara did.

She knew the first thing you needed was a medium, and that was her job. You needed quiet. You needed several participants, but you also needed the subject of the séance. And Tom was going to be that subject. The subject could be a person who was in need or could be a person with a particular affinity for the spirit world or the afterlife. Tom didn't much care about the spirit world and the afterlife; he was interested only in where the next party was on campus. But he was a good subject, Barbara had decided, and he was going to be the focus of this Friday night's séance.

She told Tom in the Student Union at Augusta College that Friday was going to be a great night for a séance; the stars were all lined up, and Mars was in the perfect alignment for the spirit world to come forward and talk to Tom. He would find everything he needed for a new beginning. Tom thought she was off her rocker, and he had no use for a new beginning, but he knew that Barbara was cute, and he was going to show up at the séance just to see what would happen.

When Tom arrived that Friday night at the séance, he found Barbara and four of her friends—two guys and two girls—and a nice large table that would serve as a setting for the séance. The lights had been dimmed. Candles and incense burned everywhere.

Barbara had dressed herself in a nice peasant dress, which was coming back into fashion, and she explained what was going to occur. They would all sit around the table. There would be some nice music that would alter the atmosphere. They would all join hands, and Barbara would help Tom focus on the parallel dimension of the spirit world. There, she would help him on a path of discovery, and he would find out what he needed to do to truly understand his life.

They all sat around the table, and they all joined hands. The music was pleasant enough, Tom thought; the typical sort of New Age stuff you might expect from somebody like Barbara. The candles flickered and burned. The incense was a little overwhelming, but Barbara had opened the windows, so every now and then, Tom caught a breath of fresh air. If you were to ask Tom how he was doing as they all sat quietly there holding hands, he would have told you he was a little bored.

But in just a minute, he wouldn't be bored any more.

All at once, Barbara's head dropped. When she raised it again, she started singing. It was an old English or Irish hymn she was singing a cappella. It didn't match the New Age music, but Tom couldn't help but think that he'd heard this hymn before. She sang the same verse two or three times, and then the song trailed off, and her head dropped again.

Her head came up. She began speaking in some strange language. The girl sitting next to Tom leaned over and said that it was actually Cherokee Indian language, and they had heard Barbara speak it before. Apparently, a Cherokee Indian was Barbara's spirit guide. This continued for a few moments until the spirit guide's voice dropped off. Barbara's head lolled forward, and everything was silent. Then her head came up, and, with a smile on her face, she said, in a voice not her own, "We have a friend here, someone who's in need of self-discovery, someone who needs to try something new, who wants to understand his difficulties and make something of his life."

Tom was a little taken aback by this, but he figured that Barbara, as an experienced séance medium, probably had the ability to do different voice characterizations. So he didn't think too much of it.

Then the voice started telling the circle things about Tom's upbringing that Tom hadn't told anybody: details about his brother who had died when he was younger; details about his father and his drinking problems; details about his mother's favorite perfume, called Lilies of the Valley. All that sent a cold chill through Tom's spine. Could it be that someone was actually communicating through Barbara from the spirit world?

It was then that candles on the periphery of the room began to flicker. Some of them actually blew out. As the smoke floated to the ceiling, the candle in the center of the table started to flicker even higher. Then the voice said, "Tom, you should follow your goals. You shouldn't let things confuse you. You're too confused."

Tom felt like the air around him had grown thick. His skin felt like something was touching him all over. He wasn't sure what was going on, but at this point, he was scared. He hadn't told Barbara much about his upbringing, but had she betrayed him? Had she done some research? Had she made some phone calls? Was it possible she'd gotten in touch with some of his closer friends and relatives back home and found out things about him that he didn't want anybody to know? Tom couldn't explain it, but he felt humiliated. He wasn't sure what was going on, but as a tingle mounted on his scalp, he knew only one thing: he was feeling very, very weak.

Then, all of a sudden, Barbara went silent.

Tom looked over his right shoulder, and standing between him and the opened window behind Barbara, he saw a young woman. The woman was very attractive, but she was dressed in out-of-date clothes, the kind of thing you might find at a consignment shop somewhere in Augusta. She seemed very young and very frail. She was looking over her shoulder out the window. Then, all of a sudden, she turned, looked directly at Tom, and said, "Where's my husband? Is he back from the war? My baby needs his father."

Tom was transfixed. He didn't know what to say. There was a ghost standing not four feet from him, and he didn't know what to do. Could he accept this idea that there was actually a dead person standing right there talking to him? He didn't know what to say to the phantom.

37

And then she asked him again, "Where's my husband? Is he back from the war? Please tell me. My baby needs his father."

Tom was confused. He had no idea what he was supposed to do next. Everyone else at the table had their eyes closed, and Barbara's head was bowed. She wasn't saying anything. And the only candle left burning in the room was the one at the center of the table.

He decided to accept the fact that maybe there was indeed a ghost standing just feet from him, no matter how strange it seemed, and so he said, "What's your name?"

She repeated again, "Where's my husband? Is he back from the war? Please tell me. The baby is crying for his father."

Tom said it louder, wondering if anyone else at the table could hear him, "What's your name?"

She said, "My name is Mattie Walker, and I'm looking for my husband. Is he back from the war?"

Tom said, "I, I don't know if I can tell you that. I don't know if I can answer your question."

And then Mattie said, "If not you, then who?"

Tom said, "I don't know."

And she repeated, "If not you, then who?"

Tom said, "I don't know when he's coming back from the war."

And then the ghost said, "If not now, then when?"

Tom turned away from the specter. He was really frightened now. He had no idea what he was supposed to say. But then the ghost of Mattie Walker kept repeating, "If not you, then who? If not now, then when?" She repeated it again. And again. And again.

Tom became terrified. Barbara was still holding his right hand, and she squeezed it very tightly, her head still resting down, her eyes still closed.

Finally, the ghost of Mattie Walker began to cry. "Where's my husband? Is he back from the war? If you can't tell me, then who can? If not now, then when? My baby, my poor son." She continued to weep.

Then, drawing courage from a place Tom couldn't explain, he turned and looked at the ghost. Was he seeing a vision, or was he seeing something real? Was he seeing a hallucination, or was he seeing something real? He couldn't tell.

"Where do you come from?" Tom asked.

The ghost turned and pointed out the window toward the other end of Augusta College, toward another cemetery on the opposite side from the Augusta Arsenal cemetery. It was the Walker family cemetery where several members of the family who had died during the War Between the States had been buried. Was Mattie Walker one of the people interred at that family cemetery?

"Is that where you come from?" Tom asked.

And the ghost just continued to point and repeat, "If not you, then who? If not now, then when? Please help my baby find his father."

Tom thought about all the people who had lost family members during the Civil War. He thought about how they were buried all over the South. He thought about the Union and Confederate soldiers buried side by side at the Augusta Arsenal cemetery, not far from where they were having the séance. He thought about the Walker family and the woman, Mattie Walker, who claimed she was looking for her husband and whether or not he was back from the war. How long had she been waiting? Where was her husband? What had happened to their son? Was he buried in the area or was he someplace else?

He decided to tell the ghost that he would help her find her husband. He would help her find where he was and where he had died after the War Between the States. He was resolute, more resolute than he had ever been before. He was able to focus and concentrate. The ghost looked at him and smiled. Here he was, an English major from Akron, Ohio, going to school in the South, and he had just made an agreement to help a ghost find out what had happened to her dead husband.

He decided to take the initiative, and he addressed

the circle that made up the members of the séance. "I'm going to help Mattie Walker now. I'm going to help her find her husband. I'm going to help her find out what happened to him during the war."

It was then that Barbara, the medium of the séance, took a deep breath and lifted her head and then released Tom's hand. Everyone else in turn began to release his or her hands, and the circle was broken. Someone at the end of the table got up and turned on the lights. Barbara looked exhausted and didn't know what had happened. In fact, none of the people in the room could recall anything.

Tom told everyone at the circle what he had seen, and they were all very excited. But when he told them that the ghost had said, "If not you, then who? If not now, then when?" everybody at the table remembered that they had heard those exact words. But they didn't think they'd heard them with their ears; they thought they'd heard them in their minds.

It was at that point that Tom decided he was going to find out what had happened to Mattie Walker's husband, and he was going to find out what happened to him in the war.

After that night, Tom Scott was different. He was very successful in school. He passed all his tests. Studying was easy. He partied a lot less, and that emotional insecurity that had been buried beneath the surface of his personality, well, it was replaced by a resoluteness, a focus, and a true security. He was able to draw on his resources. He was inspired by his unconscious. And every day, he trusted his intuition. And every morning when he woke up and said his familiar phrase, "Today, I trust myself," it meant a lot more.

Every day, for more than four years at Augusta College, Tom researched Mattie Walker and the many men who died during the Civil War. He pursued his research with a passion.

During his final year at Augusta College, before he received his degree in English, Tom discovered a long-lost ancestor who had settled in Akron, Ohio, after the war. The man's original name was Scott Walker, and he was an officer in the Confederate States of America and had been captured in battle. He'd spent time in a northern prisoner-of-war camp. While incarcerated, Scott Walker happened onto an old friend from Augusta.

This prisoner told Scott that northern raiders had killed his young wife, Mattie, and their son, Robert. Scott Walker was devastated. After the end of hostilities, he couldn't bring himself to go back to Augusta. Not wanting to see his beloved South ravaged by carpetbaggers and the ignominy of defeat, Scott Walker hung himself from an apple tree.

But his wife and son had not been killed as he has been told. Many years passed before news of the suicide reached Mattie and Robert Walker. Mattie died from grief a few years later, leaving eighteen-year-old Robert to fend for himself. Robert moved north, changed his name, and started a new life in, of all places, Ohio. Tom was beginning to understand why he had chosen to attend Augusta College. It turns out that young Robert changed his last name to Scott in honor of the father he never knew. Robert Scott was Tom's great-great-grandfather.

There was another séance before graduation, with Barbara acting as medium and Tom once again serving as subject. During it, the ghost of Mattie Walker was called. When she asked, "Where is my husband? Is he back from the war?" Tom was able to tell her everything: where he had settled and what had become of him. Tom explained to Mattie that she was his great-great-grandmother.

Mattie cried but was very grateful to Tom. Now, at last, she knew what had become of her beloved husband. Mattie promised that she would be with Tom for the rest of his life, helping him whenever he needed help, guiding him with female intuition. She would provide him with insight into the eternal cycle of life, living, growth, renewal, and rebirth. She would also tell tales of Scott Walker and the glorious years before the War Between the States.

Tom is a writer now, and whenever he sits down to create, he calls upon Mattie Walker, who shows up and guides him unerringly in whatever direction she thinks he should go. Tom is very happy. After all, not many writers have a family connection to the past who appears to them from the beyond.

Augusta's Haunted Pillar

Augusta's Haunted Pillar

Longtime residents of Augusta, Georgia, talk about a haunted pillar in old downtown Augusta. Stories vary as to why it's haunted. Some say that an African slave schooled in the occult died there rather than be sold to the highest bidder. Others talk about the gaunt preacher who cursed Augusta's wicked populace from the pillar. Shortly afterwards, a freak storm arose and destroyed everything in the area except the pillar. Still others report feeling weird sensations when near it and hearing strange sounds that seem to emanate from the very brick of the pillar itself.

There are even more sinister and tragic stories about it. But the true story of one local musician underscores the reality of one world interfering with another.

Paul Don had only wanted one thing in life, namely, to be a musician. From an early age, he showed a tremendous talent for the guitar and for entertaining people. He also seemed to possess an uncanny ability to express even the deepest feelings in song. Sometimes he played songs written by someone else, but most often he played original material, and his audiences loved it. Paul was a charmer. Night after night and song after song, he enthralled anyone who came to listen to him. For years, his reputation built until he was solidly established as one of the best singer/songwriters in the Southeast.

Then, for some reason, Paul began to lose the magic, and the crowds that came to see him and hear him play got smaller and smaller. They just weren't as moved as they once had been. Paul knew the reason why. He'd always been in touch with his feelings and emotions, which were the source of his musical inspiration, but he hadn't always been the master of them. Lately, he just couldn't "get it out," as musicians say, and he began to resent his gift and the audience.

Anger simmered just below the surface, and it would sneak out during his performances. This was the beginning of the end; no one liked an angry artist for very long. His musical opportunities began to dry up, and fewer and fewer venues wanted the volatile artist. For the very first time, Paul wondered if perhaps he'd thrown his life away.

Some months after a lackluster performance at the outdoor music festival in Birmingham known as City Stages, Paul found himself in Augusta, Georgia, visiting an old friend. As they strolled down the street, his friend, a fellow musician named Bill, said, "You'll get the groove back, man. Don't worry about it."

"That's easy for you to say," replied Paul. "You're not

the one who blows up and yells at his audience."

"I know, I know, but you just need a rest. That's all."

Needing a rest was not a new idea to Paul. Actually, he was tired all the time, and it was something more than age that exhausted him. He had lost his inspiration, and that was death to any artist.

"Look," Paul said, "I'm grateful for the gig you've arranged for me. I won't let you down."

"I hope not. This club owner's a friend of mine," Bill quickly said. Then he added, "Behave yourself, will you?"

Paul nodded. The last thing he wanted to do was disappoint an old friend—again.

The pair took a few more steps before Paul stopped abruptly and stood bolt upright. Bill turned and looked at him and said, "Are you all right?"

Paul didn't really know how to answer him. For some unknown reason, Paul felt better than he had in months. He took a deep breath and held it. A few moments later, he exhaled and said, "Bill, where are we?"

"We're where Fifth and Broad Street meet in downtown. What's going on?"

"I don't know, but for some reason, I feel, well, at home. And my head's not as foggy. Basically, I just feel good."

Paul's friend told him that there was nothing to feel good about in this particular part of downtown Augusta.

It was then that Bill pointed out the ten-foot tall brick and concrete pillar that interferes with the passersby on the sidewalk.

Paul felt strangely attracted to the oddly placed edifice. He was about to reach out and touch it when Bill grabbed his arm, pulled him back, and then motioned for him to look around. Paul noticed that the people who bustled by were carefully avoiding getting too close to the pillar. Some appeared to be afraid to even look at it. Bill, holding Paul back at a discrete distance, began recounting the history of the pillar.

It had been part of Augusta's old farmers' market built in the early 1800s. The market was the center of Augusta's commercial life for almost eighty years. Townspeople gathered there to conduct business of all kinds, some of it less than savory. Cotton, sugar, slaves, and many other things were bought and sold at the market place.

Once, a wandering preacher cursed the residents for running him out of town. As he saw it, he had come to the city to help them mend their wicked ways, but the city fathers saw it differently. To them, he was just an impediment to free trade. Before he was roughly escorted to the city limits, the preacher said that he would call down the hand of God to punish the city. "Nothing," he proclaimed, "will be left except this stone pillar as a reminder to the city to mend its evil ways." His curse came true.

A short time later, in February of 1878, a freakish winter tornado completely destroyed the farmers' market. The only thing left standing was the pillar. The preacher had warned that after the catastrophe, the pillar—God's reminder to the residents to avoid sin—should never be touched. Yet, with the passage of the years, people forget. From time to time, attempts at removing the pillar resulted in the violent deaths of the individuals who tried it. Several times, the city hired contractors to destroy the pillar. Each time, the person overseeing the project died unexpectedly. On one occasion, two workmen were hired to simply remove the pillar and carefully relocate it. Unafraid of old wives' tales, they began the removal. They were immediately struck down by a bolt of lightning that came from a clear blue sky.

Bill told of people he knew who had accidentally bumped against the pillar as they passed by it and how they were suddenly taken violently ill. "One guy," he said, "ran his car into the pillar for no reason. He wasn't going fast enough to do any real damage, but when the cops got to him, he was stone dead behind the wheel. They say he died of a heart attack, but nobody around here believes that." He added, "It doesn't pay to mess with a wrathful God."

It was then that Paul realized what was going on. The haunted pillar had fed on his anger. That's why he'd felt better when he got near it. That's why he was attracted to it. His strange attraction to the pillar wasn't an accident. It had called to him, or more precisely, his rage. Paul felt nauseous and dizzy. Had he really become such an angry person that he felt an affinity for this monument of death?

Paul asked Bill to get him out of the influence of the pillar as soon as possible. The two old friends moved down the street and sat at a restaurant so Paul could collect himself. Now, blocks away, Paul noticed that his nausea was gone. But he was keenly aware of the emotional struggle within him that had taken such a toll over the past months.

Yes, there were cosmic laws, and he thought about the trouble you could get into when you violate them. He'd been a fool to take his musical gifts and his success with audiences for granted. He'd been a bigger fool not to recognize just how much anger was actually bottled up inside of him. He'd worried about his career too much, and the resulting inner struggle had produced an anger that could be felt, not only in this world, but also in the next.

Paul decided to stay in Augusta, his career now being revived. He was more relaxed about things and cultivated a more philosophical view of his musical life. His growing fame took him all over the city, that is, except for one place. He never went near the pillar on Fifth and Broad Street again.

The Shackles of Saint Simon's

The Shackles of Saint Simon's

Esther Marshal loved to be alone with her thoughts. If she were at home right now, she'd be happily engaged in household chores. Instead, she was sitting quietly at a secluded spot of Saint Simon's Island reflecting on her new job.

For about a month, she'd been cold-calling people in an effort to sell time-shares of luxury condominiums. It hadn't gone well. She'd received virtually no training in phone sales, and her boss wasn't interested in providing any. "Just make the calls, and make the sale!" he would bark.

Esther made the calls, but she wasn't selling very much. In fact, she was the lowest seller at the office. Oddly, she didn't blame her boss for being a jerk and manipulating her into this dead-end job. Instead, she accepted the responsibility herself. She'd always been a sucker for a sales pitch, even if it sounded too good to be true. Most people would have quit by now, but Esther was made of sterner stuff. She'd promised her jerk boss that she'd give it three months, and she meant to keep her word. She had faith that it would all work out, and besides, she really liked her new apartment. And the scenery of the coast was infinitely more interesting than the view in her hometown of Macon.

Esther had visited most of the popular tourist spots in the area, but she liked the beach at Saint Simon's the best. The Atlantic waters off Saint Andrew's Sound seemed to speak to her. The rhythm of the waves made her happy, and the peaceful sound it created pushed the phone bank from her mind.

She was watching the waves wash over the beach when she noticed something protruding up from the sand. When she walked down to investigate, she saw an old rusted piece of metal. She couldn't make out what it was, but it had a slight curve to it, near as she could tell. When Esther pulled it up, she discovered that it was wide and round and connected to a length of old chain. As she pulled the object completely out of the sand, she realized what her discovery was, and it chilled her to the bone. It was a set of ancient slave manacles.

Esther wrapped her find in a beach towel and headed toward her car. As she made her way home, she wondered if the manacles might be worth something. Certainly they were as a piece of southern history, but Esther was thinking about how much money they would net from the right antique dealer. If she cleaned them up, they might fetch a nice price. "Yes, a little extra cash would be great," she thought to herself.

When she got home, Esther tossed her prize on the kitchen table and checked her phone messages. The boss was calling her to come in and work an extra shift, and he wasn't being very nice about it. Esther quickly cleaned herself up, got dressed, and headed for the office. By the time she'd settled into her workstation and dialed her first prospect, she'd practically forgotten about her find on the beach.

Eight long hours later, Esther dragged though the front door and immediately kicked off her shoes. As she headed toward the refrigerator for a refreshment, she glanced at the kitchen table and noticed that something was amiss. The slave manacles were gone. The towel they had been wrapped in was still balled up on the table, but the rusted iron and sand-coated restraints were nowhere to be found.

Could she have been mistaken about where she'd put them? A search quickly revealed the manacles in the kitchen sink. Esther was, after all, going to clean them up—maybe she'd put them in the sink before she dashed off to work. She really couldn't remember. Now, though, she had time to rinse off and clean up her beach treasure. She turned on the water in the kitchen sink and reached in and closed the drain. Then she turned around and grabbed a towel to dry off her hands. When she turned back to look in the sink, it was empty.

Esther was frightened, but she deliberately tried not to show it. Was someone watching her? Was someone in the apartment with her? She felt a presence in the small efficiency, even though her eyes told her that she was alone. She began to frantically search through her rooms looking for who—or what—might be moving the heavy artifact around. She found the manacles on the floor by the front door.

Esther stood near motionless for several minutes until she gathered enough courage to pick them up. With trembling hands, she gingerly gathered up the cuffs and chain. Then she checked the doors and windows in her apartment to make sure that she was safely locked away inside.

When she was satisfied that she was the only living thing in the apartment, she examined the manacles in more detail. Finding no clue to the bizarre happening in the cuffs themselves, Esther decided to do some research on the Internet. Perhaps she could find out more about the history of the slave trade in and around Saint Simon's Island. Before going online, Esther put the manacles in her cedar chest and securely locked it.

There was far more information available about the Georgia slave trade than Esther had imagined. Colleges, universities, and civic groups had gathered most of it. There was also a wealth of data from private individuals who did research as a hobby and posted their findings on individual web sites. Most of these people had ancestors directly involved in, or affected by, the now-despised practice of selling human beings.

One web site was created by the living descendant of a first mate on a slave ship that had once docked on Saint Simon's Island near what is now known as Dunbar Point. It detailed the story of Africans called Eboes, sold into slavery by their own countrymen. The story detailed how they were cruelly shackled to the deck of the ship.

They were human cargo, forced to travel from their native land to a strange one where they would be sold for profit. Many of them died en route from exposure, disease, and the brutality of their captors. The ones who did survive the journey to Saint Simon's were lined up on the deck of the ship and marched down the gangplank to be sold.

Consumed with fear that their captors would eat them, they ran from the slavers and dove headlong into the water. One after another followed suit until dozens had drowned, pulled under by the weight of their leg irons. As they died, so the account goes, they chanted and prayed aloud, saying, "Water, you brought us here; water, you take us home."

Esther looked from the computer screen toward the locked cedar chest. "Could this be a set of leg irons that pulled one of these men down to his death?" she thought. There was no way she could answer that question now. It was very late, and she was getting exhausted. She decided that she'd read enough. Tomorrow, she would sell the leg irons to an antique dealer and be done with it.

As Esther made a cup of tea and settled into bed, she wondered if she would have nightmares. She also said a silent prayer, thanking God for allowing her to live in a time and a place that had the good sense to abolish such a horrendous practice.

When she awoke the next morning, Esther felt refreshed and relieved. As she stared upward toward the sunlit ceiling of her bedroom, she listened to the sounds of birds singing, children, and the inevitable traffic noise.

Indeed, she was far away from the dark history of a bygone era, and that made her very happy. It was time to get up and get dressed, she thought, take the antique leg irons out of the cedar chest, and put all of this weirdness behind her. But the manacles were no longer in her great-aunt's cedar chest. When Esther sat up in bed, she saw the iron restraints resting on top of her bedspread. In fact, the rusted chain was draped over both of her ankles. She shrieked, pulled her knees to her chest, and sat very, very still.

Later that morning, Esther stood on the same stretch

of Saint Simon's beach that she'd stood on the day before. It didn't seem quite as peaceful as it had yesterday, and she knew why. The slave chains she clutched were part of a bygone world that, frankly, she didn't want to know any more about.

Most people's knowledge of history only goes as far back as the year of their birth. It was that way with Esther. To go further back to the distant past, though, meant learning things that perhaps you never really wanted to learn. Esther was changed, not because she had visited the past but because the past had visited her.

As she threw the manacles back into the Atlantic surf, she remembered the slave chant and said softly, "Water, you brought these here; water, now you can take them home."

Life Is Like a Rose

Life Is Like a Rose

Geena Freeman took delivery of the armoire at half past six on a Friday evening. For some reason, the cartage company had a hard time locating her Atlanta townhouse. They had an even harder time getting it up the two flights of stairs to her bedroom. By the time they had positioned the wardrobe against the wall opposite her bed, the furniture movers were ready to call it quits and get their weekends started.

After she had thanked them, Geena went back upstairs to inspect her new acquisition. It was an unusually large armoire with ornately carved appointments, and even though it was much too large for the room it was in, Geena was glad to have it. The armoire had been in her family for years. The last time Geena had seen the wardrobe, it had been sitting in her great-grandmother's house in Oakdale, Louisiana, where it had been for many years. Geena even remembered playing around it as a young girl.

The wardrobe had been only one of dozens of pieces of antique furniture that were in her great-grandmother's house. Actually, it would have been more appropriate to say "stored" there. Geena's great-grandmother was an avid antiques collector, so much so, in fact, that her house was a clutter of furniture, lamps, and statuary all jammed together so as to make it impossible to display any of it. Geena remembered that a pair of large art deco black panthers sat on either side of the armoire, which itself had been stuffed with all manner of antique linens and clothes.

After her great-grandmother's death, there had been some trouble with one of Geena's great-aunts who tried to snatch up all the antiques for herself. But cooler heads prevailed, and the furniture was divided up amongst existing family members. Big Mama, as her great-grandmother had been known to the family, had always said, "This is Geena's closet." And now here it was.

Geena smiled, remembering her great-grandmother. Big Mama was a courageous woman, filled with vitality and the love of life. She also had a peculiar thirst for knowledge. She could tell you the history of every antique that she had in her house, including who built or manufactured it, where it had come from, and the families who had owned them before her. But in all those years, Geena couldn't remember Big Mama detailing anything of the wardrobe's history.

Still, the piece was beautiful even if she didn't know where it had come from. Geena had never seen a piece of antique furniture with such attention to detail. Carved flowers, birds, and forest scenes worked their way up the sides of the armoire. It had two large doors that opened up to reveal one large drawer on the right side and two smaller drawers on the left. The bulk of the space was suitable for hanging coats and clothes of all kinds, including full length gowns and dresses that were worn by well-to-do women of a bygone era.

Geena couldn't remember why everyone in her family assumed that the armoire had come from New Orleans. Perhaps it was the fact that wardrobes of this kind were so immensely popular in that city. At one time in old New Orleans, property taxes were levied on homes according to how many rooms they had. Even closets and kitchen larders were considered taxable rooms.

The residents of the Crescent City began building homes without closets and used large armoires to store their clothes as a means of avoiding excessively high taxes. Big Mama used to say, "If you want a good armoire, don't go to Paris; go to New Orleans." It would probably be worth a call, Geena thought, to my parents to see if they know anything of the history of this piece of furniture. Somebody in the family had to know where it came from. Geena decided that she would call her parents later on that weekend.

Geena went to the grocery store to get what she needed to make a late-night supper. She also picked up a small bouquet of roses for her bedroom, inspired by those that were ornately carved on the armoire. When she got home, she arranged the roses in a vase and brought them up to her bedroom and placed them on her nightstand.

"There," she thought. "That brightens the room up a bit." Then she headed back down to the kitchen to make herself a late-night sandwich. Geena, moving down the stairs, was unable to notice that the roses had begun to rapidly wilt. By the time she made it to the kitchen, all of her fresh roses had unexpectedly and rapidly withered and dried.

When Geena reentered her bedroom some hours later, she was shocked to see the wilted roses. It was as if the hand of death had reached out and touched them. "Never buy flowers in a grocery store," Geena thought as she removed the vase.

She came back into the bedroom armed with a rag and a bottle of furniture polish and set to work cleaning the armoire. Removing two of the drawers was easy, but one of the smaller ones seemed stuck, as if it were catching on something. Geena wrestled with it for about a minute before the drawer pulled free. Then she saw what had been jamming it. An old journal filled with handwritten notes and newspaper clippings had been stuffed behind the drawer. Geena recognized Big Mama's handwriting immediately.

As she began to leaf through the journal, Geena realized that it contained a detailed account of the history of Woodlands Manor, a large Italian-style villa in northwest Georgia. Woodlands had been the home of Godfrey and Julia Barnsley and their descendants. It was also the home of the Barnsley Curse. "Wow!" Geena thought. "A curse—how wild is that?" It appears that Geena's great-grandmother had made an extensive study of the Savannah couple, as well as the mysterious happenings that became a part of their life and their death.

Julia was the beautiful daughter of a Georgia shipping tycoon and his overbearing wife. Godfrey Barnsley was a handsome young English cotton broker. The two were married in 1828. They were the toast of Savannah high society. Several fortunes were made and lost by Godfrey over the next few years. The pair lived in England for a time before returning to Savannah in 1830. By then, they had one child named Anna, and she would be the first of seven Barnsley children.

In 1838, his wife weakened from childbearing and afflicted by consumption, Godfrey decided to build the home that he and his beautiful bride had always dreamed of. Perhaps here, he thought, Julia could regain her health, and then they could live out their years in happiness. But it was not to be.

Godfrey bought nearly 400 acres of land in northwest Georgia that had once belonged to the Cherokee nation. Legend has it that the spirit of the spider brought the alphabet and language to the Cherokee people, so they could effectively communicate with one another. The spider spirit also showed them how to enter the spirit world by precisely writing certain letters and speaking certain words in the language that he brought to them. With these gifts, the Cherokee explored the depths and far reaches of the shadow worlds.

As Geena read on, she began to feel an odd numbness in her fingertips that slowly crept through her fingers and across the backs of her hands. She paused and looked at her left hand, inspecting it front and back. She could gain no clue to the faint numbness that was now creeping into her forearms. She decided that she was obviously clutching the book too tightly, so she relaxed her hands and her shoulders and continued reading Big Mama's journal entries.

While Godfrey was surveying his new land, he found what he thought was the perfect place for the new manor house. The site was a high bluff with a beautiful view of the property. Of course, he would have to level the bluff off and prepare the land for construction. It was then that an old Cherokee Indian who lived on the land approached Godfrey and told him that he must not build his house on the bluff. "This land is sacred," he said, adding, "Our ancestors are buried there. They will not let this happen."

Godfrey Barnsley didn't want to offend the old Indian, but his plans were not about to be delayed by the superstitions of savages. He politely announced that his decision was final and that was to be the end of the matter. Speaking in his native tongue, the old Cherokee immediately cursed him. Shortly thereafter, the Indian simply vanished and was never heard from again.

The Barnsleys moved into a log cabin on the property, which they named the Woodlands, while their new home was being built. Living in a log cabin was hard on Julia, but the promise of a grand manor in such a beautiful wooded area was enough to make it worthwhile. However, the cold winters took their toll on Godfrey's beautiful wife. She died of consumption in the winter of 1844. The curse was beginning its work.

Geena found herself getting unusually sleepy. Her eyes wouldn't focus on the old journal entries. She decided to put the book away and call it a night. "Great-grandma," she said, "you'll just have to wait until tomorrow morning." With that, she put the old journal back in the wardrobe, securely closed the doors, and prepared for bed. She had no trouble falling asleep.

Geena dreamt wildly that evening. The images and

events in her dreams were detailed and confusing, with one dream bleeding over into the next. She had dreams where she was fulfilled and happy, where she was experiencing gratitude to people she had never known before, where she was having surprising and enriching encounters with strangers. Her perceptions seemed to be heightened in her dreams. She could hear things she wouldn't normally hear and see things she wouldn't normally see. Mostly, her dreams were blissful, and she felt her heart overflowing with love, deep affection for everyone and everything in the whole world, and then ... dreams of dread and death.

Geena drifted in and out of the darker dreams, until one felt so horrible and so real that she woke up, calling out to the empty room. She sat up and turned on the light on her bed table so she could collect herself and let the bad dreams pass. As the dim light filled the room, Geena saw that the wardrobe was open, and instead of being empty, it was filled with a miasma of refracting light and light wisps of smoke that resembled clouds. All of a sudden, Geena felt very cold, the kind of cold that doesn't have anything to do with the temperature of the room, but a feeling as if the warmth in her blood and bones was slowly being drained away.

Cautiously, she got out of bed and, wrapping the bedspread over her shoulders against the cold, she approached the open armoire. As she got closer to it, she saw scenes fading in and out in the swirling mist. Geena saw pictures of woodsmen felling trees. She saw carpenters framing a house, while other people dug in the earth and cleared land. It was then that Geena realized she was watching the construction of the Woodlands.

As the scenes and images changed, fading in and out, overlapping one another, she saw Godfrey Barnsley overseeing the construction. She saw him and his wife, Julia, going over plans, making decisions, and designing the gardens and grounds of what was to be their home. She saw exotic plants and flowers and grandiose gardens that wound in curving paths all through the property. She saw boxwoods and exotic trees being planted in unique formation, and, most of all, she saw roses— hundreds and hundreds of rosebushes dotted the estate in and around the Woodlands.

They were beautiful, Geena thought. It looked like a combination of old English and Italian gardens. In the swirling mist that filled the armoire, she saw curving lines and meandering paths everywhere, just the kind of place a couple deeply in love would hold hands and stroll for hours.

Then she began to witness scenes of sadness. She saw the sadness of Julia and the children while Barnsley was away on business. She saw Julia in the throes of her illness, suffering greatly, but still clinging to the dream of the Woodlands. Finally, she saw the death of Godfrey's wife and experienced the tremendous grief felt by the man. Images of the half-completed estate and the construction falling into disrepair floated before Geena's eyes.

She then saw images of Godfrey Barnsley in a different city, possibly Mobile or New Orleans, sitting at a large table during a séance. She saw Godfrey crying and speaking emotionally to some unseen force in the room.

"He must be talking to the spirit of his dead wife, Julia," Geena thought. And then the scene changed again. In some of the clearest images in the vision so far, Geena saw Godfrey Barnsley walking with the ghost of his wife through the finished Woodlands Manor. Godfrey was talking freely with his wife's ghost. In fact, he was consulting her spirit often and regularly on all manner of decisions. Godfrey would speak to the spirit of his wife and then relay messages from her about the house, grounds, construction, and upkeep to another man who was obviously a carpenter and handyman, or caretaker, who would then follow the instructions to the letter.

The scenes continued to change. She saw for a brief period what looked like a British flag flying over the estate, and she saw soldiers of the Union army ransacking and destroying much of the Woodlands. She felt Godfrey's pain and, surprisingly, Julia's as well.

The room got colder. She saw scenes of death and illness, of despair and longing, all of it suffered by members of the Barnsley family. Geena wondered how many years were actually going by, and then she saw Godfrey Barnsley dying in poverty in the ruins of his estate.

All of a sudden, she felt colder, colder than she'd ever felt in her life, and then she was thrust backward toward her bed. The doors of the armoire slammed shut. Geena then saw the image of a young man standing before her, leaning with his back against the armoire. This apparition appeared more real than anything she had witnessed so far. The man she saw was something more real than a dream, more solid than a hallucination. The ghost was motioning with his hands to something or someone that Geena couldn't see. His arms and hands were outstretched as if trying to stop something from happening, and she could hear him say, "No, no, Preston, no—don't shoot!"

Then Geena heard gunfire and saw bullets careening off the armoire, creating little splinters of wood, while other bullets hit the wall behind the armoire. Then she saw one of the bullets find its mark as a blood stain slowly expanded on the shirt of the ghost in front of her. The wounded man slowly collapsed to the floor. A woman appeared and bent down to help the man. She was weeping. The bleeding man died in her arms as other Barnsley ghosts stood around them and witnessed his passing.

The vision was getting thinner now and less distinct. For the first time, Geena noticed that the sun was coming up outside her townhouse. As the last vestiges of the death scene faded away, the woman cradling the dead man in her arms looked up directly at Geena and said, "Life is like a rose."

No images, light, or mist could be seen now, only an open, empty armoire with a journal resting quietly inside remained. Geena realized that she had witnessed those last scenes while she was sitting shivering on the edge of her bed, but now warmth started to fill her body again. She could feel a rebuilding of her life's energy coming up from somewhere deep inside of her. For some time, she was afraid to move, but as her body temperature increased, she let the bedspread slide off her shoulders, and she stood, walked forward, and picked up her great-grandmother's journal.

That morning, she was reading in detailed prose the events she had seen in pictures the night before. She read about the life and death of the seven Barnsley children.

She read about the two who had served in the Confederate army. There were detailed accounts of each of the Barnsley descendants, including one named Preston, a prizefighter who fought under the name of Knockout Dugan. He loved the family home and used his prizefighting fortune to keep Woodlands alive and vibrant.

Preston fell into madness toward the later years of his life and had to be committed to an asylum. Later, escaping from the asylum, he made his way back to Woodlands, where, armed with a pistol and consumed by paranoia and his madness, he shot his brother, Harry Barnsley. Harry died in the arms of Godfrey Barnsley's granddaughter named Addie, and if the vision was to be believed, in the company of all the other deceased Barnsleys.

As she continued to read, Geena discovered that the caretaker she had seen in her vision had the last name of Freeman and was indeed one of her ancestors, in fact, her great-great-grandfather. That's why the spirits had been reawakened, she thought. That's why I had the vision.

Geena closed the journal and sat quietly for a moment. Almost instantly, she knew what she had to do. She decided that she would send the armoire back to Woodlands Manor.

Two months later, the museum at the restored Barnsley Manor, located in Adairsville, northwest of Atlanta, received a beautiful armoire with ornately carved flowers and woodland scenes. It had been donated by one Geena Julia Freeman, who had some distant connection to the Barnsley estate. Along with the donation was a detailed synopsis of everything Miss Freeman had learned about the armoire, condensed from the research of her great-grandmother. It appeared that the donor suspected that Harry Barnsley, Preston's brother, had been shot and died against this armoire. She detailed her sources and evidence, and after she signed her name, she wrote below her signature the motto of the Barnsley manor, "Life is like a rose."

Back in her Atlanta townhouse, Geena smiled at what must be going through the minds of the people who ran the Barnsley museum. Of course, she kept Big Mama's journal and all of the clippings. After all, it was part of her history, just like the armoire. She hadn't been able to discover if her ancestor had actually built the armoire for the Barnsleys, but she suspected it. In any event, he had been a friend and caretaker to the Barnsleys, and now she was able to continue the family tradition by returning the cherished piece of furniture to the family it belonged to.

Geena's great-grandmother had given her the gift of the wardrobe, but the most important gift was the journal itself, and not what was in the journal, but what could be read between the lines. Geena had discovered that death and destruction must occur if life could begin anew. She thought about what the Barnsleys had risked, moving to the wild woodlands of northwestern Georgia, and how they had conquered it.

That was advice you could use at any age: you have to risk, you have to conquer, if you ever expect to grow. She also knew that divine power, whether it comes from God or the Cherokee spirit world, sometimes can destroy as well as it can create.

The Ghostly Professor

The Ghostly Professor

The campus of the University of Georgia at Athens has long had a reputation for being haunted. In fact, it's almost impossible to go anywhere in Athens without stumbling over one ghost story or another. Most students who graduate from the university remember seeing at least one ghost while they were there, but one troubled student saw far more than most.

A hard rain fell on the city of Athens. It was the kind of pocket thunderstorm that frequently pops up during the summer months. One minute, there was heat, humidity, and blue sky, and the next, intense cloud-to-ground lightning, thunder, and lots and lots of rain. Hal was stuck out of doors under the awning until it passed.

Hal van Horn was a recluse who didn't fit in at all at the University of Georgia. He hadn't made many friends at school due in large part to his unwillingness to try and make any. In fact, he had worked very hard to stay separated from other students as well as the faculty. Hal was the kind of person who would tell you, rather quickly, that he didn't need friends and acquaintances. He'd rather linger on the fringes of college life and be alone.

The rain continued to fall. The campus was largely deserted, this being the Fourth of July weekend. Hal had no interest in visiting his parents, and he liked the idea of having free run of the huge college campus. Sure, there were other students on campus, but not nearly as many as are usually there when school is in full swing. Here, he could practice the fine art of being by himself.

As he sat on the concrete bench under the awning, musing about the rain, a girl approached him from underneath a walkway. Her hair looked wet, and she'd obviously been caught in the cloudburst, but now she was seeking the shelter of Hal's awning. The attractive girl sat down next to Hal and said hello. He politely returned the greeting.

She introduced herself by saying, "Hi, my name's Persephone, Persephone Spring."

Hal thought to himself that her parents were probably ex-hippies to give her such an outrageous name. But then, his name wasn't very common either. "Pleased to meet you, Persephone. I'm Hal van Horn."

Persephone smiled and said, "Hal, you don't have any books or a Walkman or anything. Are you just sitting here enjoying the rain?"

Hal responded by saying, "Well, actually I was just walking through campus, enjoying the fact that there weren't very many students here, when the cloudburst started. I just had to keep from getting wet." He then added, "I really like it when there's not many people on campus."

"Really?" replied Persephone. "There's a lot more people here than you can possibly imagine."

Hal wasn't sure what she meant. Most folks cleared out for the July 4th weekend, but she was cute and pleasant enough that he was willing to let the conversation continue. Besides, she seemed to be one of the only interesting girls he had met in months.

As the two continued to chat, it became clear that Persephone was grilling him for personal information, but Hal wasn't having any of it. He was keeping his emotions, his feelings, and details about his personal life pretty close to the vest. It's best not to reveal too much too soon, especially to a strange girl.

Although Hal wasn't quite sure how they got started on the topic, he found himself lecturing about great philosophers in the western tradition. He had spent hours and hours reading Nietzsche and Heidegger and analyzing their ideas. For some reason, he was telling all of this to Persephone. He was about to launch into a discussion of why Kierkegaard was so misunderstood when Persephone gently reached up with her hands and touched her fingertips to his lips. He was a little shocked by this, but she obviously wanted him to stop talking.

Then Persephone said, "Hal, what do you care about?"

As shocked as he was, Hal responded almost instantly, "Well, I care about being alone. I'm not really all that comfortable around people, particularly large groups of people, and I'm not so sure I'm all that comfortable telling you about it."

Persephone then asked, "Do you feel different than everyone else?"

"Yes," he responded, "I care about things that none of these people seem to care about."

"So you don't like other people very much?" Persephone asked.

"No," replied Hal, "their lives get a little bit too dramatic, and they wallow in the details of their tawdry little existences."

Persephone laughed, and Hal nervously joined in. He was still chuckling when she said, "Fair enough. Now, let me ask you another question. What do you fear?"

At that point, Hal was silent. He was definitely not comfortable talking about his fears, and it was this kind of questioning and intimacy that had kept him from many a relationship. But he managed to say, rather timidly, "I'm afraid of large groups of people. That's why I like being alone. Sometimes there's so many people on this campus, I feel like the ground itself is just going to open and swallow me whole."

"Mostly," Hal said, "I'm afraid of people forcing themselves into my life."

Persephone then said, "Listen, Hal, I'm sorry to be so inquisitive, but you see, I'm a teacher here at the university, and I've been here for a long time. I can tell when a student is in trouble, and you are in trouble. You don't pay much attention to the clothes you wear, and I bet you couldn't even tell me what you had for dinner last night. By the way you're dressed, I can tell that you're kind of disorderly and that your mind is scattered. And I bet you misplace things all the time."

"Why should you care?" Hal asked. "I'm not in any of your classes."

"Hal, I care because if you're not careful, you're going to turn into an emotionally bland person. Your personality will become flat and featureless until, frankly, you won't have one at all. Then you might as well just be dead."

The subject of death wasn't a new one to Hal van Horn; he'd thought about it often. He would at times feel so different and removed from everyone else that he thought he would just be better off if he left this world and just moved on to the next. But now, to have this strange girl talking to him this way, he was afraid of the subjects of death and dying.

"Say," he asked, "what subjects do you teach anyway?"

But Persephone Spring continued to talk as if she hadn't even heard his question. "I have to introduce you to some of the lesser known faculty here at the university. They have great lessons to teach you. I think just about ten lessons should do the trick. Can you count backwards from ten to one, Hal?"

"Of course I can. What has that got to do with anything?"

"Don't argue," Persephone said, "just start counting down from ten."

Not quite sure where any of this was going, Hal looked up, said, "All right," and in a loud voice he proclaimed, "Ten, nine, eight, seven, six, five, four, three, two, one!" Persephone Spring leaned forward, pursed her lips, and gently blew a puff of air in Hal's face.

The sound of his own voice was still reverberating in his ears when the whole scene in front of him changed. He was no longer under an awning, waiting out a summer thunderstorm. He was sitting in a round garden with people moving around in it. The grass was wet, and the sun was trying to shine through dense clouds. Persephone was sitting next to him with her hands folded on her lap, her eyes closed, and a smile on her face, when out of the garden came an old Confederate soldier.

He approached the couple sitting on the bench and

looked at Hal specifically. Then he motioned to four broken swords he had dangling from his belt. It was at this point that Hal became very clear that he was looking at a ghost. Then the old soldier spoke: "Everything isn't fine, do you hear me? Everything is not fine: it's an illusion. This truce, this truce—it's a sham peace. It isn't real. It's the calm before the storm."

Hal opened his mouth and tried to speak, but before he could say anything, the old Confederate soldier said, "I'm not a coward! I'm not a coward!" and he clutched at a crucifix around his neck. It was in fact a St. Andrew's cross, and it hung from an ornate gold chain. Hal wasn't sure what any of it meant, but the old Confederate soldier turned and walked away, repeating over and over again, "It isn't fine; everything is not fine. It's an illusion, a sham peace—the calm before the storm."

As the old soldier walked off to the right of the garden, Hal could see a juggler standing in the center. He stood on what looked like a raised mound of earth, and in his hands he juggled a cup, an old Civil War saber, an egg, an arrow, and four large gold coins. But before Hal could focus clearly on the juggler, a tall, gaunt woman walked in front of him. She was wearing a blue-green dress decorated in lace, and she walked slowly and evenly on her tiptoes. She was carrying two things: a party mask and a small dagger with a crescent moon engraved on the handle. She would periodically take the mask and put it to her face as if she was remembering Mardi Gras for just a moment, and then she'd remove it again.

She approached Hal and said, "Justice, my son, balance and sober perception, that's what you need. You must realize your responsibility in everything that you experience. Don't think too much; your mind will freeze up on you, and then your face will become just like a mask." With that, she turned and, deftly on her tiptoes, slowly walked away.

Something caught Hal's attention to the left. It looked like a portly old man in what appeared to be clothes from the 1800s. He was stomping paper on the ground and other items that you might find on a desk. "It's all ruined!" the old man said. "It's time to put an end to this thing, break it off completely, make a clean sweep, and start over! I don't know why I started this project in the first place, but it's time to stop it now, just to stop it altogether!" With that, he continued to stomp up and down on the papers and desk accessories that were under his feet.

It was at that point that Hal realized he was counting under his breath. He had said the word "three" when he saw the old man. He must have said "two" when the woman appeared and counted the Confederate soldier as "one." But he couldn't remember counting the juggler.

Persephone leaned into him and touched his shoulder and said, "Come on, now, Hal; say the next number," and Hal found himself whispering, "Four."

As soon as he did, he found himself standing at a table. Stretched out on the tab were four empty cups. Each cup had something different engraved on it: fulfillment, gratitude, partnership, and celebrate were the words of that adorned the four empty goblets. He was bending forward to look more closely at them when all of a sudden the juggler walked up and said, "I'm lesson number five," and stood between Hal and the table. Then the juggler picked up the cups and began to deftly toss them in the air.

The juggler wasn't standing on the little mound of earth any more. The juggler danced in front of Hal and then said, "Oh, no, my boy, you've got to be resolute—concentrate now, concentrate! Life gets pretty tricky, and it's your job to fill these up! You have to trust in your own abilities. But you have to study, and you have to pass tests! Fill these goblets up! That's at the center of it! Willpower! Vital force! Discipline! That's what you need, my lad!"

And then he danced off.

Then Hal heard Persephone whisper the word "six."

Hal saw a series of spinning disks in front of him.

They shifted and changed from one side to another, one disk blending with another to make a larger one. They spun and shimmered light that radiated out in all directions. Hal wasn't sure where the light was coming from, but he was transfixed.

Persephone then said, "Hal, if you understand this, then you can make a change for the better, and you'll be surprised—your perceptions will lead you, and it will be very, very wonderful. Quickly now, say the next number!"

Hal resolutely said the word "seven," and he immediately felt happy, blissful. He hadn't been to church in years, but he realized that trusting in God might be a good idea. He didn't really have a profession, but he longed for the day when he had a job that he would enjoy. And at that moment, he felt a deep affection for everybody, and he kind of wished all the students were back on campus.

"Have courage," Persephone said. "Say the number of the next lesson."

They said it together: "Number eight."

Nothing specifically happened when he uttered the number, but he heard Persephone speak in a voice that was more clearly than any sound he had heard in his life. "Hal, you've got to learn to risk something. You have to get worked up about something. Be passionate. All of life is a suspenseful game between dominant and devout forces. A macho behavior isn't going to do, but you can be too sensitive as well. You have to trust yourself. You have to have an eagerness to fight for something that you believe in."

Hal's head began to spin. He wasn't able to think clearly, and he felt like he was falling. He didn't have the opportunity to say the number nine, but he knew he thought it, and when he did, everything took a turn for the worse. He felt weak and unclear, and he thought himself as being a complete failure.

How much had he hurt himself by being alone all of the time? Was he facing total destruction? He felt like he was falling down a flight of stairs. When he hit bottom, he felt utterly defeated. But then, as he lay there, he realized that he'd been avoiding conflict constantly his entire life, and he understood how that was causing great strife, not only to himself but also to those people around him.

Then he heard Persephone say the word, "Ten!" and she clapped her hands.

Suddenly Hal's eyes snapped open as if he had just awakened from a dream, and there the pair was, sitting on the bench underneath the awning. The rain was beginning to let up, and sun was trying to shine through the clouds. He turned and looked at Persephone, his teacher for the last few minutes, though he had no idea really of how much time had passed. And he realized the truth of things. He'd heard stories about the many ghosts that walked the campus at the University of Georgia, but he had never believed any of the stories, and he certainly never expected to meet one. Today he had met several.

But Persephone wasn't the kind of ghost who carried her head underneath her arm and floated in and out of the student union. Nor was she the young man who died accidentally at one of the fraternity houses. She was a teacher, and she was the kind of teacher that Hal had wanted to meet his entire life. She was the kind of teacher who could speak to you directly, no matter who you were or how emotionally distant you made yourself.

"Hal," she said, "you have to go out and make some friends. I know you have problems with authority, but your desire for solitude is blocking your development as a person. There's no need to get angry. There's no need for any sort of a struggle between people. You just need to relax and let life happen to you. Don't be so intolerant. Try not to suppress your anger all the time. You have a lot of uncontrolled and unchanneled energy, and you're not going to find any secrets in your philosophy books. You have to get out and actually do something with your life."

"I've enjoyed our time together," she said.

With that, Persephone took a deep breath and then, pursing her lips again, gently blew a puff of air in Hal's face. He instinctively closed his eyes. But when he opened them, Persephone the ghostly teacher was gone.

"Wait, wait!" he said. "Who were these people and where did they go?"

He heard Persephone's voice say, "Each of these people died in and around this college campus, but every human being has something to teach. If they can't teach it in life, then they endeavor to teach it in death. Haven't you ever had the feeling that someone was telling you something you couldn't possibly have known? Did you ever feel as if you were receiving wisdom and knowledge that was coming from unseen quarters? Well, that's how ghosts teach. We show up where we're needed, and we do what we need to do to get our lessons across. You've just had ten of them."

"Am I going to see you again?" Hal asked.

And then he heard a voice say, as if it came from the raindrops falling off the roof and the branches and leaves onto the ground, "You have to let me go now, but I'll be back. After all, this is college; I am a teacher. And you still have so much to learn."

The Phantom Rider
of Mystic

The Phantom Rider of Mystic

John Cuthrie had known old May Allen his entire life. She had been a friend of John's mother when he was young. After his mother died, May didn't come around as much, which pleased John. Young boys generally don't like being around old women, and John was no exception. Also, May Allen reminded him of his mother, and he preferred not to relive the painful memories of her death.

John's mother and May Allen went to the same church, and sometimes he would attend Sunday services with them. The two women were shape-note singers at the small southern church outside Mystic, Georgia.

Shape-note singing was a simplified approach to singing church hymns. Even though it was praise music, John thought that the shape-note hymns had an eerie quality to them. Everyone sat on elevated pews arranged in a large square and engaged in call and response with the hymn leader. Frequently, that leader was May Allen.

May's late husband had given her an expensive diamond necklace with a matching set of earrings that she wore to church every Sunday. John thought that the jewels were much too fine for May, and, as a small boy, resented her for flaunting them. After all, his mother could never have fine things and neither could most of the people in their small rural church. John felt that May Allen had no right being so high-hat.

May Allen's other prized possession was an old hill pony named Red. The two were inseparable. No matter where old May was, Red was never very far behind. Even after May was too old to ride, she would drive down the road in her old car at a snail's pace with Red trailing close behind. Whether it was Sunday services, the market, or their small town post office, you'd see Red tied to a hitching post wherever May was doing business.

John and Red liked each other at first, but horses have a sense about people. As John grew into a discontented and angry teenager, the old pony began to keep his distance. When John would approach him, Red would snort loudly, turn sideways, and paw at the ground with his front hooves. John got the message and stayed away. Soon, he disliked Red as much as he disliked May.

As John grew up, he had numerous run-ins with the local law. These were small offenses at first and nothing of any consequence. Later, though, his offenses turned into real crimes, and soon everyone in and around the community of Mystic considered him a menace. "Bad seed" they called him.

Before too long, John had had enough of the town of Mystic, and he decided it was time to leave forever. The last person who saw him before he left was old May Allen, who chastised him vigorously for ruining his life. She said, "Your mother would be brokenhearted to see the mess you've made of things. Straighten up and act like you've got some sense!" In response, John said some very unkind things and then he left.

To a young man, forever isn't quite as long as he thinks it's going to be. So it was fifteen years after he'd "gone for good" that John found himself back in Mystic. Life in the big city hadn't been what John expected, and things had gone from bad to worse for him. He'd even spent some time on a county prison farm. Unfortunately, John's experiences hadn't taught him anything about the straight and narrow. Instead, he was a bitter man who came back home because, frankly, he didn't know where else to go.

Old friends and neighbors knew nothing about John's life of crime after he'd left Mystic. They were hoping only that the years away from home had mellowed him and tempered his anger. Little did they know that John was already contributing to the increase in petty crime within their community.

Old May Allen had died two years after John left town. Red, her constant companion, refused to eat after her death and died a short time later. Some say he died from grief. Red just could not stand to be separated from his beloved mistress. The part of the story that was most interesting—to John at least—was that May Allen had been buried in her expensive jewels. John visited May's grave, not so much to pay respects to his mother's best friend, but to get the lay of the land. John, you see, had decided to rob the grave and steal the diamond necklace and earrings.

John picked the night of the next full moon to commit his crime. If the weather cooperated, he'd be in and out of the cemetery and halfway to Atlanta to sell the jewels before anyone noticed.

Now grave robbing is a nasty business at any time, but on this hot summer's night, John found it particularly difficult. It was very hot and humid, and he was covered in sweat before he dug his first shovelful of earth. An approaching thunderstorm threatened to make it much worse, so John wasted no time.

The earth was reasonably moist from a wet and rainy spring, and it made the work go quickly. Soon John was engaged in a continuous rhythm of digging. He paused once to keep his eye on a slithering snake. The light of his lantern illuminated the snake as it moved along the edge of the grave. From time to time, he would catch glimpses of a predator's eyes in the night underbrush.

Occasional flashes of lightning in the distance silhouetted the headstones and memorials. He was most disquieted by the sounds of thunder that seemed to resonate through the ground itself. The claps of thunder sounded much closer to John than they should've been. He looked up to see just how far away the approaching storm really was and then continued to dig.

Periodic blasts of hot breeze on his face and neck reminded John of the hot summer days of his youth. Those memories were not pleasant ones. He pushed them aside and kept digging. Amid the sounds of shoveling earth and the approaching storm, John thought he heard something moving among the tombstones. Though he could see nothing, John couldn't shake the feeling that he wasn't alone.

Suddenly, John felt his shovel hit something solid, and he experienced a rush of adrenaline. He continued to dig until the coffin was uncovered. Soon thereafter, he used a crowbar to force the simple wooden coffin open. There before him was the rotting corpse of May Allen with her jewels glittering by lantern light. Moments earlier, it began to lightly rain, but John hadn't noticed. The thrill of discovering the diamond necklace and earrings pushed everything else from his mind. John, beginning to be covered in mud, set to work removing the jewels. He began by removing earrings from lifeless flesh. John was surprised that the sight of his mother's dead friend hadn't bothered him very much. Earrings in hand, he turned his attention to the diamond necklace. "Give it up, Worm Food," he said aloud as the necklace came free.

It was raining harder as John pulled himself out of the open grave. For several minutes, he inspected his prizes by the light of his lantern. He marveled at how the jewels glistened in the light. Then he felt the ground shake as a clap of thunder rumble all around him. A blast of hot breeze pushed through the rain and broke John's reverie. Quickly, John put the jewels in his pants pocket and, glancing one last time at the corpse of May Allen, he headed toward his car to make his getaway.

It was a good twenty-minute walk to where he had hidden his car, and as he made his way through the rain and the woods, for the very first time, John felt afraid.

Petty theft, assault, arson, vandalism—John could now add grave robbing to his list of dubious accomplishments. He put his hand in his pocket and fingered the diamonds to make sure they were still there. Satisfied that they were secure, he quickened his pace and began to run through the woods. Then, abruptly, John stopped and surveyed the woods behind him. "Is someone following me?" John thought. But no matter how hard he looked, he could see no one. It was raining harder now, and the ground shook with thunder. It was as if the storm was following him trying to thwart his escape.

Ten minutes later, it occurred to John that he must have taken a wrong turn on his way back from the cemetery. Five minutes after that, he realized that he was probably lost. John stood still in a small clearing. Holding his lantern high, he looked around trying to decide where he was. Suddenly, from somewhere behind him, he heard a loud noise that sent shock waves through his spine. The sound was the scream of a wild animal and was something between a panther's howl and horse's neigh. Whatever it was, it was large, and it was getting closer.

John Cuthrie's feet were virtually stuck to the ground. No matter how hard he tried, he couldn't force his legs to move. Rustling in the woods and brush behind him signaled the approach of something—something fearful, something large. Then a large shape leapt out of the woods and knocked John to the ground as if he were nothing more than a dead branch.

John looked up to see the ghostly shape of a horse standing before him. The animal lifted its head, screamed again, and reared up on its hindquarters before stomping the earth. With each stomp of its hooves, the ground shook. The ghostly animal snorted a blast of hot sweet breath, and John realized that the unseen presence he had previously felt was now standing before him. The thunder had been its hooves, and the hot breeze had been its breath, the breath of death! The sight of the spectral beast illuminated by flashes of lightning frightened John, but there was something familiar in its movements. Then fright turned to terror as he recognized the sideways twist, snorting, and pawing of the horse. It was the ghost of May Allen's horse, Red.

The phantom horse snorted and reared upward again before charging John, who scrambled to his feet and ran for his life. "He knows what I did to May's grave. He knows I have the jewels," he thought. Red was almost upon him, so John dodged in and out of thickets in a vain attempt to evade the vengeful horse.

Red's ghost charged through the trees and underbrush. The horse struck at John with his forequarters but John kept running. No matter where he ran, though, Red stuck to him like glue and was never far behind. John could feel the sickly sweet aroma of its hot breath on his neck. With each blast of breath, fear tore at John's soul.

The next few minutes seemed like hours as their game of cat and mouse continued. Finally, John hid behind a large tree and listened for sounds of his pursuer. All John could hear were the sounds of the woods and rain. He remained still and didn't move. For the first time in years, John Cuthrie prayed.

After a few minutes had passed without any sight or sound of his adversary, John thought it safe enough to step out from behind the tree. When he did, he found himself standing face to face with Red's ghost! The horse gave a quick jerking turn of his head and, with an unearthly snort, knocked John flat on his back. John looked up in abject terror to see a rider upon the horse. He wiped the mud and sweat from his eyes. John was staring at the rotting corpse of May Allen sitting astride her beloved pony.

May's corpse got down off Red and slowly walked toward John. "My God!" he thought. "She looks just like she did when I left her in the grave." Covering his face with his hands, he screamed in desperation. Red stepped closer and pawed thunderously at the earth several times.

"What do you want from me?" John asked.

A reply hissed out of May's black and yellow teeth. "My jewels," she said, "give me back my jewels."

John frantically searched his pocket for the diamond necklace and earrings. For a brief moment he feared that he might have dropped them during the pursuit. Finally, he felt the jewels. He tossed them to the ground between May's corpse and where he lay, as if they might form a barrier to her approach. Rotting flesh and bone picked up the jewels and put them back where they once had been.

May stood up straight as if she were admiring the jewels in a mirror. Earrings hanging on dried flesh and a necklace surrounding exposed bone presented a morbid and surreal picture. Then the corpse looked at John with vacant sockets and hissed, "Your mother would be brokenhearted to see the mess you've made with your life. What are we to do with you, John Cuthrie?"

It was then that John heard himself begging for his own life. He promised to mend his ways and be a better person. He would make it up to the people of Mystic any way that he could. "Please," John cried, weeping uncontrollably, "please don't kill me!"

The ghostly pair stood over him, silent and near motionless. Then May Allen hissed, "See that you do, young man." She turned and mounted Red. Dead horse and rider disappeared into the woods. As they did, the sound of thunder faded away and the breeze cooled.

The next morning, John staggered out of the wet and rainy woods, exhausted and in shock. In the days that followed, the town buzzed with stories about poor May Allen's grave being desecrated. It was collectively accepted that a transient had been the culprit and was long gone by now. The townspeople were relieved that May's diamond necklace and earrings were still on her body and had been untouched by the grave robber. Two days later, May and her jewels were re-buried in a brand new coffin. John didn't go to the service, but he was certain that May did, indeed, have her jewels again. He also knew that no one but May would ever have the necklace and matching earrings. She and Red would see to that.

Though he was never able to fully tell anyone in Mystic what had happened to him that night, no one really cared. You see, John is a different man now. He's happy and contented for the first time in his life. He spends his time farming and raising horses. Oh, he also sings in the church that his mother attended when he was a child. It seems that John Cuthrie has become quite an accomplished shape-note singer.

The Bleeding Lion

The Bleeding Lion

It had been more than an hour since the three friends had stolen into the graveyard to do some mischief. Now they were running nervously through the Oakland Cemetery trying to get away from whatever might be stalking them.

"What are we running from?" Matt said.

"I don't know," replied Carol, "but we can't seem to shake it off our trail."

"Wait a minute!" added Phil. "Are you sure that we aren't running from our own shadows? After all, it is dark, and we are in a cemetery."

The trio paused to consider whether or not they had spooked themselves in this eerie place. They nervously glanced left, right, and all around while trying to catch their breath.

"Do you still have the paint?" Carol asked.

Matt answered, "Yes, I've got the paint, and quit asking me, all right? I'm not sure how you two managed to talk me into this crazy stunt, anyway. It'd serve you right if I took off and left you guys here by yourselves."

"You wouldn't get very far," Phil said, "because I've got the keys."

All of a sudden, the friends heard a twig snap in the bushes. Flashlights swung around in a vain attempt to illuminate the cause of the sound. They could see nothing.

"Okay, this is creepy," Matt said. "Let's find this 'dead rebels' monument of yours so we can get out of here."

"It's not my monument!" snapped Phil, adding, "I hate the thing."

"Oh, come on Phil. You've never even seen the monument. How can you hate something that you've never seen?" Carol chastised.

"My father hated it, and that's good enough for me, so shut up!" he replied.

Phil Corrigan's father had always been ashamed of his family's Civil War heritage. A distant relative had fought and died for the Confederacy and was buried in the very cemetery he and his friends now found themselves.

To Phil's dad the southerners of the Civil War era were cowardly traitors who were better off dead. Over his lifetime, strangely enough, he had grown to despise the idea of them as people. Civil War history became an unhealthy obsession, and he never tired of talking about it to anyone who would listen. But no matter when or where he was talking or whom he was talking to, Phil's father slipped into an anger-filled screed peppered with anti-South rhetoric. Soon, no one wanted to listen anymore. On his deathbed he rambled on angrily about the monument to the brave confederate dead at the Oakland Cemetery in Atlanta. "Dirty rebels don't deserve a monument!" he said. He died a hate-filled man. Unfortunately, he passed on his irrational hatred to his son, Phil.

Phil and his trio of friends planned to spray paint the monument with graffiti as a weird kind of tribute to his father. But the would-be vandals couldn't find the monument and were beginning to lose their nerve.

"Okay. Let's split up," Phil said. "Whoever finds it first, just sing out, and we'll get to work." He added, "It's got a dead lion on top. You can't miss it."

As the three fanned out in different directions, Phil couldn't fend off the nervousness he was experiencing. It was a good idea to separate; best not to let Matt and Carol see him like this.

Phil wasn't having much luck finding the monument. He stopped for a moment to get his bearings when he heard a commanding and mysterious voice call out someone's name. Then he heard the response, "Here!" echo through thin air. The mysterious voice called out another name. This time the reply of, "Present!" reverberated around him. Another name was called out and another and still another. Each time the called name was followed by a ghostly response of "Here!" or "Yo!" or "Present, sir!"

"Oh, my God!" Phil thought. "The ghosts are taking roll call!"

Then the mysterious voice called out the name "Jerimiah Corrigan." At the sound of his last name, Phil let out a loud shriek and turned to run away, but before he could take more than two steps, he tripped and fell face first on the wet grass.

As he pulled himself up from the ground, Phil saw the monument he had been looking for. Atop a seventeen-foot high base reclined a marble statue of a great lion weighing more than 30,000 pounds. A spear thrust into his chest mortally wounded the lion and his paws clutched the fallen flag of the Confederacy.

Phil stood up and examined the memorial in the beam of his flashlight. The ghostly roll call continued to ring in his ears, but his gaze was focused on the stone lion. Here before him was the object of his father's hate. Here was the monument to the unknown dead of the Confederate army. Phil was transfixed.

Phil heard the sound of Matt and Carol approaching and was about to call out to them, when his eye caught sight of subtle movement on the statue. He took a step forward to get a closer look at the origin of the movement. He saw it immediately and wished he hadn't; red blood was dripping freely from the stone lion's chest wound! Phillip Corrigan dropped his flashlight, turned, and ran toward his friends. He grabbed them by their arms, urging them to run—and run they did.

The trio disappeared into the night never to return to the tomb of the Confederate Unknowns. But if they ever did, they would still be able to hear the ghostly roll call of the dead. They might even see the huge stone lion breathe, weep, and bleed for the lost souls the majestic beast protects for all eternity.

The Phantom Flagman

The Phantom Flagman

For most of Simon Everett's young life, people had told him that he was the best youth minister they had ever met. He could talk to just about anyone, and even the most troubled teens found it easier to communicate with him than they did with their parents. More importantly, he was able to provide real world advice and solutions to their real world problems. When somebody would occasionally praise him for his insight and wisdom, he would humbly say, "Thank you. This is what I do."

Unfortunately, being a young man, Simon had much to learn about dealing with people. Frequently, his criticism of their behavior was too harsh, and it was difficult for him to understand that it didn't do anyone any good to be too forceful. He found himself being harsh with people more oftentimes than not, and it became clear to Simon that he was having a problem.

Perhaps he was having a crisis of faith, or perhaps he just hadn't lived enough life yet to know how to really communicate with people. Whatever the reason, he decided that he needed to go on some sort of spiritual vacation to help sharpen his sense of reality. He was an energetic young man, generally imperturbable, with intense staying power as long as you stayed out of his way. But he couldn't take people disturbing him, breaking his stride, or in any way interfering with his personal rhythm. So he decided to spend time alone with his thoughts by going on a journey of discovery.

He made the decision to begin hiking the state of Georgia, leaving his hometown of Columbus. He would let the open road quicken his perceptions, and he would come to rely fully on his own strengths and his own abilities to solve problems and fend for himself. Simon Everett trusted in his ability to master any situation and to size up any person, so he knew he wouldn't have any problem as he hiked through the state.

As he set out along the way of his journey, he immediately learned to patiently trust in the natural cycles of the life he was currently living. He would dedicate himself to covering a certain amount of distance every day, and along the way, he would volunteer at area churches. Occasionally, he would preach, or maybe even stay a day or two in a town, doing work around area churches in exchange for food and board. It was clear to everyone who met him that he was a special young man who was willing to assume responsibility for his own growth and development.

As the weeks turned into months, Simon started to

gain some insight into the way he'd been conducting himself as a youth minister. He was beginning to see things that, he believed, probably ought to change. He began to have a sense that he needed to make a clean sweep of things and just, well, start over. Simon recognized that he would often get carried away in his capacity as a minister, and he began to see where his harsh criticism and forceful truthfulness came from; he was, simply, trying too hard.

Going out on the road brings the refuge of solitude where a man can think for himself, and Simon was taking full advantage of it. He was finding his sense of reality reinforced, and he found that some of the issues in his life that he thought of as problems weren't really problems at all; it was just a question of growing up. In any event, as he made his way down the road, he could tell that his journey of discovery was bringing order to his life.

One day after a particularly long hike down a lonely stretch of road, he found himself at a campsite near the town of Blackshear off Georgia Highway 38. It was a lovely little campsite, made even better by the fact that Simon was completely alone. That night, he wrote in his journal, had a meal fit for a king of the road, and experienced all the sounds and images of a spring night in Georgia. He was keenly aware of the all-or-nothing beauties of the great outdoors. He was also experiencing a sense of peace and euphoria that he had never experienced in his life. Yet at the same time, Simon almost couldn't sit still. He was on fire with possibilities for new ministries, new projects, and new ways to help people in his home church, and he furiously wrote in his journal until he just couldn't write any more.

Then he unrolled his sleeping bag, tended to the campfire, and laid down for a well-deserved night's rest. As he lay there about to go to sleep, he found his mind playing with all sorts of disconnected thoughts, and he found himself curiously questioning everything. He was playing intellectual games, doing multiplication tables and word games. He quietly complimented himself on his intellectual slyness in solving some of these self-imposed puzzles that ran through his mind there at the campsite.

But amid the feelings of euphoria and suspense in a mind alight with the possibilities of life to come, there was also a feeling that something strange was about to happen. Simon experienced a feeling of lightness or tingling on his scalp. He paid no attention to it and drifted off to sleep.

As he began to fade off into sleep, he imagined that he was tumbling and falling, as if he'd rolled out of bed. He wasn't sure, but he felt that he might be a little bit afraid, as if he was falling toward some sort of dangerous situation. But he wasn't sure. Then, all of a sudden, it felt like someone grabbed him by the hair on top of his head and pulled him right out of the sleeping bag.

When Simon opened his eyes, he wasn't yet aware that he was dreaming, but he looked down to see himself lying comfortably and peacefully in his sleeping bag at his campsite. Standing next to him was the man who had pulled him out of the sleeping bag by the top of his hair. It was a railroad flagman who smiled pleasantly and tipped his hat. In one hand, he held a flagman's lantern that was fully lit and shone light all over the campsite. He reached out and took Simon by the hand, and then the two started to walk away from where Simon's physical form lay sleeping.

Now, in Simon's ministry, he had told people not to believe in ghosts, but here he found himself in a dream—or something more real than a dream—apparently walking through a campsite with one. And then the most amazing thing happened: Simon and the ghostly flagman began to float up into the air. Higher and higher and higher they went, slowly gaining height and distance over the countryside. Soon, the campsite was in the distance. The flagman held out his lantern to illuminate the area in front of them, and Simon found himself floating with his ghostly companion over the tops of trees and houses. When they crossed roads, he saw cars and trucks pass beneath him.

Occasionally, the flagman would circle low and pay a visit to an area house. Most of the time, the people inside the house weren't aware that anything was going on, but Simon and his ghostly friend floated in and out of the attics and ceilings, visiting one- and two-story houses. Simon was astounded to see that he could actually focus on things that were on top of shelves and china cabinets. He could read letters on desks and book titles on top shelves, and even listen to the conversations as he drifted from one room to another, one house to another.

Along the way, the flagman took Simon in through the roof of an area church where they were getting ready for some sort of festivity. The choir was singing and people were making punch and generally getting ready for a celebration.

Simon and the flagman sat up in the rafters of the huge country church and just watched the scenes below. The flagman had not once said a word to Simon the entire time, and for some reason, Simon couldn't speak, either. But as he looked around the rafters of the rural church, he noticed a message carved neatly into one of the top rafters. The message read, "Dedicated to the people of Screven," and there was a date Simon couldn't make out. He was about to lean forward to get a closer look at the carved inscription when the flagman grasped him by the hand, and they both floated out the ceiling of the church and off into the night.

Simon was starting to become very uncomfortable with the whole situation. Was this a dream? If it was, how come he couldn't wake himself up? If it was something more than a dream, then it was something more than Simon had ever experienced in his young life, and it frightened him. Where was this grinning ghost taking him next?

It was almost as if the flagman realized that Simon was getting scared because he smiled, held his lantern toward the ground, and the pair floated to the earth. As they were a few feet above the ground, Simon saw old railroad tracks illuminated by the flagman's lantern. A moment later, Simon and his ghostly companion were standing on the crossties.

The flagman held his lantern high, and as Simon looked around, he couldn't make out what it was that he was supposed to see—if anything. He looked over at the flagman, who just smiled and nodded his head and continued to hold his lantern high to illuminate the surrounding area. Then, off in the distance, Simon heard the sounds of an approaching train. His natural reaction was to step off the track, but for some reason, he couldn't get his feet to move. He looked at the flagman, who just smiled and nodded his head and held his lantern aloft, while Simon desperately tried to communicate with him that they needed to get off the railroad tracks.

But still Simon couldn't speak. He looked off in the distance, and he could see the headlamp of the oncoming train. The flagman smiled quietly at Simon and then began to walk forward in the direction of the train. Simon reached out with his hands, trying to pull him back, but couldn't reach the ghost.

The train was getting closer and closer now, and the flagman began swinging his lantern from one side to the other, as if to slow the train. But the train wasn't slowing. The oncoming train got closer and closer. Finally, Simon was able to muster enough strength to shout for the flagman to get off the tracks. The flagman stopped, turned around, looked at Simon, smiled, and nodded his head, and then began walking toward the oncoming train. Simon felt the pulling at the top of his head again, as his feet lifted off of the crossties. He began to float in the air above the railroad tracks.

The fast-moving train was moments from the flagman, who continued to walk on the crossties, swinging his lantern back and forth. There wasn't anything Simon could do except look at him in horror as the train ran headlong into the flagman.

The flagman's lantern skittered to the ground, but even more horrifying was the sight of the flagman's head being knocked off his body and rolling into the brush alongside the railroad track. By then, the fast-moving train passed under Simon in a flash. Moments later, the train was gone.

The flagman's body lay off to one side of the railroad tracks near his lantern, but his head was nowhere to be found. Simon wanted to go down and tend to his new friend, but the pulling sensation at the crown of his head became more intense. Before he could prepare himself, Simon's floating body was snapped backwards like a rubber band.

In a flash, Simon found himself back in his sleeping bag at the campsite. He was covered in a cold sweat and breathing heavily. He sat up and threw off the sleeping bag. For what seemed like hours, he sat with his knees in his chest, trying to compose himself. He had a sip of water from his canteen and tried to relax.

He recorded his dream in his journal, having decided that it was, indeed, just a nightmare. The details were so vivid and the sounds and the smells were all so real. Writing the dream down in his notebook seemed to ease Simon's mind quite a bit. Soon he drifted back off to sleep and woke up the next morning to a bright and shiny opportunity for a brand new day.

He made his breakfast, broke camp, and headed off down the road. Even though the sun was shining, and Simon was feeling generally very good about himself, the events of the previous evening had left him very disturbed and uneasy. Generally, nothing could shock this young man, but today he was feeling weak and unsure of himself.

As he walked along Highway 38, an occasional train would pass by, sending chills through Simon's spine. Soon, he realized if he didn't spend some time around some friendly people, he felt he might go a little bit nuts.

A short time later, Simon found himself at Milligan's railroad crossing on what was called Bennett Road in this part of Georgia, really an extension of Highway 38. It was almost dusk, and Simon couldn't help but think about his dream the night before. Had it been real? Had it been a dream? Was that a ghost or was it just his imagination?

While Simon was trying to figure out just exactly what had happened the previous night and why he was filled with such dread, he noticed something coming down the railroad tracks by Milligan's Crossing. It was a round light floating four or five feet above the railroad tracks, bouncing slowly from one side of the railroad tracks to the other. Simon couldn't see where the light was coming from, but he chalked that up to the tricks that dusk light can play on you.

But as the light got closer, he saw that it was free-floating—no one was holding this unearthly light. The pulsating orb of light, about the size of a basketball, got closer and closer and closer to Simon. And then, in panic, Simon began to run from it. But the light chased Simon down the track, swinging from side to side, bouncing from one track to the other.

It was darker now, and the orb of light was getting closer. As Simon cleared some trees, he saw a small church and made for the front door. There were people inside getting ready for a wedding. He was grateful to see a room full of living people. Simon walked in the church, briefly turning around to see the light floating off into the wilderness that framed the railroad tracks.

Someone greeted him at the door, and Simon introduced himself. Over the next few minutes, Simon in his characteristic fashion had made friends with most everyone there. The warmth and fellowship of these people even chased away his fear. He even agreed to stay for a few days and help them with their wedding celebration and possibly exchange some room and board for some work around the small church. It was then that Simon realized that the church he was standing in looked like the church he had seen in his dream. In fact, this was the very church that he and his ghostly friend had been in the night before.

Simon asked someone, "Is this Screven?"

And they said, "Why, yes it is. This is the oldest church in the area."

As Simon was hanging wedding decorations, he maneuvered his ladder to catch a glimpse of one rafter in particular. There, just as he had seen it in his dream, was the inscription, "Dedicated to the people of Screven."

Simon stayed for the wedding and even accepted an invitation to be the guest preacher on the following Sunday. His sermon revolved around the theme of quietly holding the illuminating lamp of your faith and love for all to see.

It wasn't until two days later that Simon told the parishioners of Screven Church about the ghostly light that chased him down the railroad tracks and the dream he had had the night before. As it turns out, the ghostly lights were a regular feature of this community, and many people had seen them. There are a great many stories as to where the lights came from, but the most common one concerned a railroad flagman who, sometime near the turn of the century, tried to slow down an oncoming train and had unfortunately died in the attempt. Nobody knows why the flagman was trying to slow down the oncoming train. Perhaps there was livestock on the track or a small child was playing too close to it. But one thing everyone agrees on, when they recovered the flagman and his lantern, they couldn't find his head. And during the evenings, particularly evenings after it rains, some say you can see the flagman waving his lantern back and forth, trying to find his head.

The locals say that no one else has ever been killed on the tracks at Screven. In point of fact, because of the unearthly lights that play in the area, no one ever goes near them.

The Haunted Overpass

The Haunted Overpass

Joanne Rosen left the campus of Abraham Baldwin Agricultural College much later than she had planned. All of the other students who were going home for the weekend had left hours earlier. But Joanne had a good reason for getting a late start. She had just met with her advisor to discuss the subject of changing her major, and the two talked well into the late Friday afternoon hours.

As she headed south out of Tifton in her secondhand pickup truck, Joanne carefully rehearsed the speech that she was going to have to make to her parents waiting for her back home in Florida. "Mom, Dad," she said aloud, "I'm not going to major in agribusiness any more. I've decided that I'm changing my major to music." Her words reverberated through the cab, and Joanne shuddered. She had come from a long line of farmers and ranchers in Florida, and she was expected to continue in the family tradition.

Joanne wasn't a "girlie" girl, fond of frills and bows. She was a down-to-earth farm girl loaded with common sense, who had jumped at the opportunity to attend ABAC. While she was at college, she began playing the piano again. Joanne's mother had taught her to play

124

when she was younger, and she showed great talent for the instrument. For some reason she couldn't remember, Joanne just simply stopped playing.

But now the music bug had bitten her, and nothing would stop her. Joanne was grateful to her college advisor for noticing how much happier and contented she had become when she started to play the piano again. Still, Joanne knew, her father would feel that happiness wasn't all that it was cracked up to be. "I wonder how Dad will take the news," Joanne asked aloud.

It wasn't a long way to her home in Florida. In fact, it was just over the border, not far from Valdosta. Still, it would be a long ride as she worried about how her parents would take her news. She wasn't very far south of Tifton when she saw a girl about her age with long brown hair walking along the side of the road. "There's no reason for a girl to be walking the highway at night," Joanne thought, so she pulled over and waved to the girl.

As the walker approached the truck, Joanne offered her a ride. "Hop in!" she said. "I'll give you a lift down the road."

The girl smiled, said, "Thank you," and got in the passenger side of the truck.

As Joanne pulled back onto the road, she noticed that the girl was looking distressed in some way as she stared straight ahead. "Where are you headed?" Joanne said. "Where can I drop you off?"

Her passenger said that her car had broken down somewhere along the road here. She'd gone for help, but she couldn't find any. And now, as she headed back to the car, she couldn't locate that either. Joanne chuckled to herself, thinking it was kind of amusing that someone could misplace a whole car on a stretch of Georgia road.

Her passenger turned and looked at Joanne with a gaze that seemed to penetrate right through her. There was something unsettling about this girl, Joanne thought, and she decided to ask her a few more questions. "Do you live around here?" Joanne asked.

"No," the girl said, "I go to Abraham Baldwin Agricultural College."

"Really?" Joanne said. "That's where I'm going to school. I'm headed home to Florida right now to see my parents."

Her passenger replied, "I'm from Florida, too, but I haven't seen my parents in a very long time."

"Hey!" Joanne said, "Where are you from in Florida? Where's home?"

Her passenger ignored the question and just said, "I can't believe I lost my car. It's got to be around here someplace."

"Did you run out of gas?" Joanne asked.

Her passenger replied, "I'm not sure what happened. I'm still confused about it." Joanne began to wonder if perhaps the girl had been in some kind of accident, but her passenger didn't seem to be injured in any way.

The girl leaned forward, put her hands on the dash, and said, "Wait a minute! There it is. Just—just by that overpass." Joanne looked, but couldn't see anything resembling a broken-down car. All she could see was a sign that announced it as the Omega Road overpass.

As they got to the overpass, Joanne's passenger said, "No, wait! Stop here. There's my car." So Joanne pulled the truck over and stopped. Her passenger hopped out of the cab and ran to the overpass.

Joanne turned on her high beams and got out of the truck to follow her strange passenger. She caught up with her just as the girl said, "Look—there it is. Oh, my God! Look—there's my car." Joanne looked in the direction that the girl was pointing, but couldn't see anything. "Don't you see it?" the girl said. "Oh, look what I've done to my car. My parents are going to be so angry."

Joanne took a couple of steps forward but still couldn't see any car. There was just the overpass. Then she heard it—the sound of squealing tires. It was one, maybe two different pitches of squealing tires, and they were all coming toward her. She looked quickly behind her to see if there were any oncoming cars, and then turned and looked in the other direction. But she could see no other cars on the road, just her truck parked off to the side. The squeals culminated in a loud crash, and Joanne heard the sounds of metal being twisted, glass breaking, and the screams of a young girl.

It was then she noticed that her passenger had vanished. Where had she gone? Joanne Rosen stood silent for a second. She was standing alone on this stretch of highway. There were no crashed cars, no passenger, nothing but her truck and its high beams illuminating the overpass.

She carefully walked toward the overpass to make sure that she was alone. There were no cars; nothing that revealed the source of the squealing tires could be seen anywhere around her. And her passenger had completely vanished.

Then, all of a sudden, she heard the sounds of squealing tires again. Was it one car? Maybe two? Maybe more? The squeal was loud and went on for what seemed like an eternity, again culminating in a loud crash and the sounds of metal and glass being strewn across the road. She even heard the unmistakable sound of gravel flying in all directions. But again, no matter where Joanne looked, she could see nothing. She was alone.

She was very afraid now, but she took a deep breath and, steeling herself, began to squint at the overpass. She focused and concentrated on the empty stretch of road in front of her. Then, after a few moments of intense concentration, she began to see a picture form before her. Somewhere outside the edges of her visual perception, she was able to make out the vague image of two cars with the front ends smashed and grilles twisted, smoke rising from the engines. Tires were flat, and she could smell the aroma of burning rubber.

She approached the scene as bits and pieces of it faded in and out of her field of view. It took Joanne a few moments to realize that she was looking at a scene that was radically out of date. Both of the cars in the wreck were older models that were now completely out of fashion.

Only then did it occur to her that her passenger had also been wearing clothes that were also out of date. The vision of the wreck faded, and she rubbed her eyes and looked again, concentrating, at the road directly in front of her. The vision came back into focus; clearer than it had been the first time. She carefully approached the wreck.

As she got closer, Joanne looked at the driver's side of one of the cars. It was there that she saw the girl with long brown hair that she had picked up minutes earlier. Covered with blood and pinned by the wreckage of her car, the girl was dying behind the steering wheel.

Joanne called out to her, but the girl didn't respond. Joanne panicked. She didn't know what to do. She was witnessing the vision of a wreck that had happened years earlier. She didn't know if there was anything she was supposed to do other than just stand there and watch the scene unfold. She tried to reach out and comfort her former passenger, but her hands passed through the car and the girl as if they were thin air. Then the girl turned and looked at Joanne, and with her last breath gasped, "Help me. Please help me."

Joanne heard the sound of sirens approaching from behind her. She turned and looked over her shoulder but couldn't see anything. And when she turned back to look at the accident, the broken cars and their dying passenger were gone.

Joanne Rosen stood motionless for a few moments and just glanced around. What had happened here? An accident that fades in and out of view? The squealing of tires and the screams of the dying—here one minute but gone the next? For a moment, Joanne thought that she might be going crazy, but then it hit her: the passenger she had picked up was a ghost.

Joanne walked and then started running toward her truck, when she heard the sound again—squealing tires, one or two pitches, the sounds of a crash, and then screams. She turned and looked toward the overpass but again could see nothing. She quickened her pace, running faster toward her truck. "If I can just get back in the truck and lock the doors, I'll be safe," she thought.

She hopped in the old pickup, slammed the door, and locked it tightly, then stared at the overpass where she had seen the ghostly accident. She quickly glanced over at the empty passenger seat next to her, apparently afraid that the ghost of the dead girl might appear there again. But the seat remained empty, as empty as the road in front of her.

Joanne Rosen pulled back onto the road, anxious to leave the area as soon as possible. But then she stopped the truck. She had to go through the Omega Road overpass, and the thought of it terrified her. She gunned the engine and soon was through the junction and fifty yards beyond.

She pulled over to the side of the road, rolled down the window, and turned and looked at the overpass. There was nothing there. Could it all have been some strange dream? Then she heard it again: tires—not one but two sets—squealing, converging, a massive crash, the sounds of twisted metal and broken glass, the smell of smoke, and the screams of the dying. Joanne threw the truck into drive and got as far away from the junction of Omega Road and Highway 75 as she could.

Joanne fractured a few speed limits for the next few minutes until she pulled off to a roadside gas station to collect herself. Inside, she told the clerks what had happened and discovered she wasn't the first person to have witnessed the ghostly sights and sounds on Omega Road.

Yes, some years before a young girl from ABAC had left the college late one Friday evening and, just like Joanne, was on her way south to see her family in Florida, but she never arrived. The stories varied as to whether or not it was one car involved in the crash or if it had been a head-on collision. Other drivers on this stretch of road had picked up the girl, who had taken them to the overpass. Some of them had seen one car engulfed in smoke and flames; others saw two, while others saw three cars. No one was quite sure what had caused the accident. But one thing they all agreed on: the young girl still walks that lonely stretch of road looking for her car. She never made it home to her parents.

As Joanne Rosen continued her journey back home to see her parents in Florida, she decided that she wasn't going to discuss her decision to change college majors. She'd had enough excitement for one weekend, and she wanted the next few days to be as normal and peaceful as possible. She was, simply, going to be grateful to be back home.

That next Sunday as she made her way back to Abraham Baldwin Agricultural College, Joanne made sure to leave in plenty of time, so that she would be going through the Omega Road overpass in broad daylight. As she did, she stared straight ahead, not wanting to catch any more glimpses of the spectral car accident or its hapless victim. But as she drove away, she heard the distinctive sound of squealing tires fading behind her.

Ghost of the Werewolf

Ghost of the Werewolf

Professor Howard Wyatt was thoroughly enjoying his vacation. Sprewell Bluff State Park was the perfect place for an outdoorsman like Howard to unwind while appreciating some of the most beautiful wooded areas of Georgia.

Howard was a professor of American folklore at a large northeastern university. He specialized in folk traditions that contained gruesome tales of man-like monsters, vampires, and zombies that roam the American backwoods. In that capacity, he had created a database of dark and unusual happenings, so a complete examination of these strange events might take place in the bright light of reason.

In truth, this was a working vacation for Professor Wyatt. He was researching the local legends surrounding the Burt family of Talbot County. During the mid-nineteenth century, the wealthy Burt family made its mark on the state of Georgia between Macon and Columbus. They were one of the most elite families of the state and enjoyed all of the benefits that great wealth could bring.

But great wealth does not insure happiness, and in the mid-1840s, Mildred Burt found herself a widow with four children to bring up and raise on her own. One daughter in particular was of interest to Professor Wyatt. Isabella Burt was a very strange looking young woman. She was tall and lean like her father, with thick dark hair and heavy eyebrows that covered penetrating brown eyes. But it was her teeth that were the most disturbing to people who met her; they were sharp and pointed like a wild animal's teeth. It was so pronounced that people wondered if they had been purposefully filed to conform to the pointed shape.

Isabella was given to nocturnal fits and wanderings that went far beyond simple insomnia. Eventually, doctors prescribed opium syrup, probably laudanum, to help her sleep, but rarely did it do any good. Most nights she lived in the throes of physical torment and addiction. She spent her days in the family library seeking release from a variety of illnesses in the pages of books and the fantasy of story. It was the only thing that made her truly happy.

One winter morning, news reached the Burt household of a series of brutal attacks on sheep in the area. In each instance the sheep's throat had been torn out. Neighbors suspected a large wolf of being the culprit. As the attacks became more frequent, area farmers and landowners set out to hunt down and kill the beast. Isabella was always keenly interested in the details of each attack. As the unknown animal continued to terrorize the countryside, her interest turned into an obsession.

One night a group of farmers and gentry were pursuing the wolf. They opened fire on the wild animal, and one of the bullets found its mark. But when they ran up to the wounded shape, they discovered Isabella Burt covered in blood. The hunters were certain that they had been chasing a wolf. Isabella must have gotten in the line of fire. But why was she running barefoot through the woods at night?

Isabella lost her left hand in the attack. Some say that her mother shot her. Still others say that she was accidentally wounded by her sister and ran off into the woods. There was even talk that Isabella had been shot while attacking a family member with a knife.

Whatever the reason for the strange happenings that night, as soon as she was able to travel, Isabella went to Paris. Ostensibly, she was there to visit a distant relative. In reality, she was being seen by a doctor who specialized in treating victims of lycanthropy, also known as werewolf-ism. Individuals afflicted with this disease suffer from the delusion that they turn into a murderous wolf. But the residents of Talbot County were under no delusion. While Isabella was away in Paris, the wolf attacks on livestock ceased completely.

When she returned from Europe, a few isolated sightings of the wolf returned, also. There were even several attacks on sheep at various area farms. Only her wealth and family's standing in the community kept her out of jail. Everyone was certain that she was a werewolf that tore out the throats of her victims.

Isabella Burt lived out her years in loneliness and obscurity and died in 1890. Her exact burial place remains unknown. Some say that she is buried in the hallowed ground of a churchyard, while others say that she drowned herself in a nearby lake. Old timers say that her spirit wanders Talbot and Upson counties in the ghostly form of a wolf.

Howard Wyatt was running down a series of leads as to Isabella's final resting place. Rumor had it that she drowned herself somewhere nearby, but the professor wasn't having any luck locating the site. He had searched the area for days and talked to more people than he could count. No one he interviewed could help him, so he decided to call it quits and end his working vacation early. However, he wasn't going away empty-handed.

He had discovered the skull of a very large dog in the shallows of a nearby lake and thought that it would make a great souvenir of his hunt. He wrapped his discovery in an old pillowcase and put it in his backpack.

As he was hiking out of the park, an old woman from a nearby farmhouse flagged him down. She was having some difficulty rounding up her horse and getting him in the barn for the night. Something was spooking the horse, and she couldn't do a thing with him. Howard obliged and rounded the horse up and put him in his stall. Feeling particularly grateful, the old woman offered him a nice home-cooked meal as a way of thanking him. He wasn't about to refuse. It turned out to be the best chicken and dumplings he'd ever had.

Howard and the old woman were enjoying pleasant conversation and a cup of coffee when he heard scratching and sniffing at the kitchen door.

"I think your dog wants in," said Howard.

"But I don't have a dog," replied the woman.

She went toward the door to investigate, but before she reached it, the woman saw something that caused her to shriek. Through the window, she saw a huge creature with the jaws and teeth of a wolf but the eyes of a human being. Arms covered in hair hung low from the shoulders of the half-man, half-animal. Claw-like fingers opened and closed rhythmically, and a low growl emanated from its slavering jaws.

Howard lunged for the kitchen door to make sure that it was securely locked. The old woman grabbed a pump shotgun from the corner and leveled it at the window. One blast from the old Remington blew out the window glass and most of the frame.

Howard hid behind the kitchen table as the pair watched the broken window. Quite some time passed before either of them had the courage to open the door and look outside to see if the man-wolf was going to return. It did.

As the pair opened the kitchen door, they were confronted by a wolf with human eyes standing upright on muscular hind legs. It was only then that Howard realized that they were a woman's eyes; it was a she-wolf!

Howard quickly grabbed for the shotgun. His movement seemed to startle the wolf. It quickly turned and ran away from the house. Howard followed it taking another shot at it along the way, but the creature darted toward a nearby lake. He arrived just in time to see the she-wolf slip noiselessly into the deep waters of the lake and disappear completely.

The professor stood at the lake's edge trying to make some sense of what he'd just seen. Then it hit him; the human she-wolf was the ghost of Isabella Burt. As he had this revelation, he heard the howl of a wolf in the distance, and it chilled him to the bone. Professor Howard Wyatt ran back to the farmhouse as fast as he could.

Once inside he recounted what he had witnessed to the old woman who lived there. But when he told her about the skull in his backpack she said, "Son, you've got to get rid of that thing. Don't you see? You've angered Isabella's ghost!"

The rest of the night passed without incident. The next morning, Howard set to work repairing the kitchen window. But before that, he took the skull from his pack and threw it into the middle of the lake. As it sank below the surface, Howard heard a sound in the distance. It was the mournful howl of a wolf.

About the Author

Ian Alan is a psychic investigator and ghost hunter who has spent his life researching the enigmas and mysteries of the world. He is a teacher of ancient art and philosophy as well as a prolific free-lance writer. Ian Alan lives and writes in Birmingham, Alabama.